**Political Generations and
Political Development**

Written under the auspices of
the Center for International
Studies, Massachusetts Institute of Technology, and the Center
for International Affairs, Harvard University

Political Generations and Political Development

Edited by
Richard J. Samuels

Lexington Books
D.C. Heath and Company
Lexington, Massachusetts
Toronto

Library of Congress Cataloging in Publication Data

Main entry under title:

Political generations and political development.

Bibliography: p.
1. Political sociology—Addresses, essays, lectures. 2. Conflict of
generations—Addresses, essays, lectures. I. Samuels, Richard J.
JA76.P59   301.5'92   77-168
ISBN 0-669-01463-X

Published simultaneously in Canada

Printed in the United States of America

International Standard Book Number: 0-669-01463-X

Library of Congress Catalog Card Number: 77-168

Contents

Preface

The quest for a "key" to unlock the nature of political conflict is a persistent theme for political scientists and social theorists. Some focus on ethnic conflict, others on class conflict, still others on the tensions between institutional structures. Each of these cleavages arises under different conditions, and each can take quite different forms, particularly as a result of the kinds of issues that become salient. Several are likely to exist simultaneously within a single political system. Each has its own distinctive conceptual tools of analysis: The class conflict approach rests heavily upon economic analysis; a focus on ethic conflict tends to be more sociological, and so on.

During the past twelve years that the Harvard–MIT Joint Seminar on Political Development has been meeting, we have given attention to economic, ethnic, and institutional issues, but paid little attention to generational ones. In 1975-76, JOSPOD turned its attention to the theme of generational change. One reason, perhaps, is that most of the founding members of the Seminar have themselves moved from one generation to another and were personally familiar with the first generation of leaders that took power when independence was achieved. We were, therefore, particularly aware of the tensions that have arisen as one generation was displaced by another. The founding fathers of new states often did not retire; nor were they defeated in elections. In many developing countries they were deposed by coups, assassination, or arrest: Ben Bella in Algeria, Lumumba in Zaire, Sukarno in Indonesia, U Nu in Burma, Nkrumah in Ghana, Mahatma Gandhi in India, and, more recently, Sheik Mujibur Rahman in Bangladesh. And even when the transition from one generation of leaders to another was peaceful, the sons (or daughters) often repudiated the values, the institutions, and the policies of the founding fathers. Only in China did the generation that brought about the revolution remain in power long and become a veritable gerontocracy whose leaders maintained their authority by deposing youthful critics or keeping them under tight control.

At the mass level, the most striking characteristic of the younger generation in developing countries is how numerous it is. A rapid decline in the mortality level for infants during the past twenty years, without a correspondingly rapid decline in the birth rate, has produced a disproportionately large young population. Indeed, only a small part of the current population of most of the developing countries that achieved independence in the 1950s or early 1960s has ever lived under colonial rule or experienced the nationalist struggle. In Algeria, which became independent in 1962, only 44 percent of the population in 1975 was over the age of twenty-three—that is, above the age of ten when French rule ended. In Ghana, which became independent in 1957, only thirty-five percent of the population is over thirty-three—that is, fifteen years or older when the British departed. And in India, one of the first countries to become independent in 1947, only a fifth of the population now alive was above the age of thirteen at the time of independence. So we are talking about populations that never experienced European rule, or witnessed the struggle for independence, and whose political socialization has largely taken place in the period since independence.

The Joint Seminar this year looked at the implications of some of these generational changes both at the popular and at the leadership level. Attention was given to a number of generational conflicts, the different perceptions that arise as a consequence of generational change, the relationship between generational conflict and other forms of conflict, and the criteria for measuring generations in a number of developing countries, including Peru, China, India, Israel, and the Arab world, as well as the Soviet Union, Eastern Europe, and the United States.

Myron Weiner
Samuel P. Huntington

Acknowledgments

The editor would like to thank the staffs of the Harvard Center for International Affairs and the MIT Center for International Studies for their very professional assistance throughout 1975-76. In particular, the cooperation of Amelia Leiss, Kathleen O'Sullivan, Fran Powell, and Barbara Talhouni ensured the smooth functioning of this year's seminar. Jessie Janjigian provided patient editorial supervision, and Peter Jacobsohn helped steer the final manuscript to publication. The expert typing of Jane Tuchscherer, Wayne Wendler, and Dianne Thomure also aided in the publication of these proceedings.

Adnan Abu-Odeh, Fellow, Center for International Affairs, Harvard University (1975–1976).

Jiro Aiko, Fellow, Center for International Affairs, Harvard University (1975–1976).

John Ashworth, Graduate Student Associate, Center for International Affairs, Harvard University.

Daniel Bell, Professor of Sociology, Harvard University.

Valerie P. Bennett, Manager, Policy Analysis Department, Energy Resources Company, Cambridge, Massachusetts.

Robert R. Bowie, Professor of International Affairs, Harvard University.

Nazli Choucri, Professor of Political Science, Massachusetts Institute of Technology.

Ann Craig, Graduate Student, Department of Political Science, Massachusetts Institute of Technology.

Jorge Dominguez, Assistant Professor of Government, Harvard University.

Richard S. Eckaus, Professor of Economics, Massachusetts Institute of Technology.

S.N. Eisenstadt, Visiting Professor (1975), Department of Government, Harvard University.

Carolyn Elliot, Professor, Center for Research on Women, Wellesley College.

Minoro Endo, Fellow, Center for International Affairs, Harvard University (1975–1976).

John O. Field, Research Associate, Center for International Studies, Massachusetts Institute of Technology.

Daniel Fine, Research Associate, Center for International Affairs, Harvard University.

Nathan Glazer, Professor of Education and Social Structure, Harvard University.

Bernard Gordon, Chairman, Department of Political Science, University of New Hampshire.

*William E. Griffith, Professor of Political Science, Massachusetts Institute of Technology.

Merilee Grindle, Assistant Professor of Political Science, Wellesley College.

H. Field Haviland, Professor, The Fletcher School of Law and Diplomacy, Tufts University.

Gregory Henderson, Professor, The Fletcher School of Law and Diplomacy, Tufts University.

Cavan Hogue, Fellow, Center for International Affairs, Harvard University (1975-1976).

Raymond Hopkins, Research Associate, Center for International Affairs, Harvard University.

William Dean Howells, Fellow, Center for International Affairs, Harvard University (1975-1976).

*Samuel P. Huntington, Professor of Government, Harvard University.

Warren Ilchman, Dean, College of Liberal Arts, Boston University.

*Harold R. Isaacs, Professor of Political Science, Massachusetts Institute of Technology.

Willard R. Johnson, Professor of Political Science, Massachusetts Institute of Technology.

Nathan Keyfitz, Professor of Sociology, Harvard University.

*Martin Kilson, Professor of Government, Harvard University.

Amelia C. Leiss, Assistant Director, Center for International Studies, Massachusetts Institute of Technology.

Daniel Lerner, Professor of Political Science, Massachusetts Institute of Technology.

Bruce Mazlish, Professor of History, Massachusetts Institute of Technology.

Joel S. Migdal, Associate Professor of Government, Harvard University.

John D. Montgomery, Professor of Government, John F. Kennedy School of Government, Harvard University.

Eric Nordlinger, Professor of Political Science, Brown University.

Barbara Norwood, Fellow, Center for International Affairs, Harvard University (1975-1976).

*Speaker.

Hana Papanek, Associate Professor of Sociology, Boston University.

*Amos Perlmutter, Professor of Political Science and Sociology, The American University.

Ithiel de Sola Pool, Professor of Political Science, Massachusetts Institute of Technology.

John D. Powell, Professor of Political Science, Tufts University.

*Lucian W. Pye, Professor of Political Science, Massachusetts Institute of Technology.

*William Quandt, Associate Professor of Political Science, University of Pennsylvania.

L.N. Rangarajan, Fellow, Center for International Affairs, Harvard University (1975-1976).

John Reid, Fellow, Center for International Affairs, Harvard University (1975-1976).

Rosemarie S. Rogers, Associate Professor, The Fletcher School of Law and Diplomacy, Tufts University.

Robert I. Rotberg, Professor of Political Science, Massachusetts Institute of Technology.

Milton Sacks, Professor of Political Science, Brandeis University.

Richard J. Samuels, Graduate Student, Department of Political Science, Massachusetts Institute of Technology, Executive Secretary, JOSPOD (1975-1976).

William Schneider, Assistant Professor of Government, Harvard University.

*Alfred C. Stepan, Professor of Political Science, Yale University.

John Thomas, Institute Fellow, Harvard Institute for International Development.

Sidney Verba, Professor of Government, Harvard University.

Arpad von Lazar, Professor, The Fletcher School of Law and Diplomacy, Tufts University.

Karl B. von Pfetten, Fellow, Center for International Affairs, Harvard University (1975-1976).

*Myron Weiner, Professor of Political Science, Massachusetts Institute of Technology.

*Speaker.

1

Introduction: Political Generations and Political Development

Richard J. Samuels

Political generations involve the lives of individuals bound to each other through shared experiences of the passing of time alone, just as political development addresses the life of the society as it unfolds under the impact of generational and other sources of change. Both are clearly based on the notion of time, and therefore both must deal with continuity and change. Indeed, the ephemeral character of a "generation" presents possibly the greatest problem in using the concept in political analysis. Generations are never static in time; they are perpetually confronted by new social contexts—contexts that invite and foster competition with yet newer generations. The concepts of development and generations are inherently dynamic; the study of both necessitates historical investigation. For this reason it is surprising that they have not yet been paired in a crossnational context within a single volume. Bringing them together is the purpose of this collection.

Like many analytic constructs with significance for political study, the concept of political generations is a product of sociology. It has seldom appeared in the political science literature, and even more rarely has it been utilized in the writings on political development (except, for example, Ashford [1963] and Quandt [1969]). Rintala (1968) has pointed out how generations was a concept popular in the arts and in cultural histories even before its theoretical formulation in the sociological literature. In the social sciences the idea of generations has been addressed by numerous sociologists, and most perceptively by Karl Mannheim (1928), Kingsley Davis (1940), Ralph Linton (1942), S.N. Eisenstadt (1956), Joseph Gusfield (1957), and Bennett Berger (1960). But this initiative by sociologists by no means precludes the potential application of the concept of political generations to political science in general or to developmental studies in particular.

Samuel P. Huntington, in his contribution to this volume, sketches the three dominant models of political generations. The first generational hypothesis, that associated most closely with the work of Karl Mannheim, suggests that shared politically relevant experiences among members of the same age cohort is the necessary condition for the shaping of a generation. In this view the political values formed by particular historical experiences become the enduring part of a youth's intellectual orientation as he enters the adult world. Mannheim (1928) argues that "mere chronological contemporaneity cannot of itself produce a common generational location" (p. 297); what is required for the formation of an identifiable generation is "participation in a common

1

destiny" (p. 303). Sigmund Neumann (1939, 1965), Rudolf Heberle (1951), and Ralph Linton (1942) have shared the view that adult values are generally formed out of events experienced in early adulthood and which inform the individual's *Weltanschauung* for the rest of his life. Moreover, they agree that within any society there are clusters of individuals who have commonly experienced such events and that these clusters can influence the course of politics.

The second generational hypothesis that Huntington identifies is most closely associated with the early work of S.N. Eisenstadt (1956). Eisenstadt's is a structural-functional model of individual development in a stable society. In his view individuals' values change as they proceed through the life cycle. Their youthful rebelliousness is tempered by the demands of adult life, and in time their adult roles change and shape their social and political orientations. Eisenstadt sees the smoothly functioning society as the one that allocates roles in part on the basis of age, and thus as the individual ages, his roles change. In this model, therefore, political orientations are seen as temporal. They may initially be formed as a response to an established order, but they give way as youths adjust to adult society. Lipset and Ladd (1972, p. 67) briefly trace the intellectual history of this life cycle or maturational model, and they find evidence of its nascent formulation in Aristotle's *Rhetoric* and in the essays of Max Weber.

In considering these two dominant models we are left with what might be called the paradox of the generational hypotheses. The life cycle model suggests that initial political orientations, formed from youthful protest, are transitory and pass away as adult roles bring the maturing person into the social mainstream. The experiential model stresses instead the enduring character of certain fundamental orientations derived from shared events and assumes that adult roles are generally chosen to conform to these previously established norms. The paradox appears because the two models treat continuity and change in opposite ways at both the individual and the societal levels. At the individual level persistence is associated with the experiential model while change is associated with the maturational model, but at the societal level precisely the reverse is true. In the experiential model identifiable age cohorts that possess various orientations that are consistent over time succeed each other and thus they change the distribution of values in the society (Inglehart 1971; Butler and Stokes 1971). On the other hand, the maturational model suggests that while individual orientations are transitory, the dominant values of the society are enduring. Thus, in this model, social change is minimal whereas individual change is maximal. In the experiential model individual change is minimal after the initial formative experience, but societal change is more likely. Several of the contributions to this collection, most notably those by Huntington, Kilson, and Griffith, examine the implications of each model in their case study.

Huntington also identifies a third generational model, the interaction model, which sees generational conflict as rooted in each generation's reaction against the values of the previous one so that there is a cyclical nature to social and political change. Unlike the life cycle model it does not posit ephemeral protest. It suggests, on the contrary, that reaction becomes the stamp that identifies a generation even as it itself ages. It is not unlike the notion of dialectic change as applied to political orientations and identification. Kingsley Davis (1940) was among the first sociologists to ask why the rebelliousness of youth in Western society is so marked in comparison to elsewhere.[a] He suggests that such generational conflict is due to one or more of several factors. In Western society the rate of social change is high, and therefore the prior socialization of parents occurs in a different social context than that of their children. This leads to conflicting social norms. Davis also suggests other differences between parent and child such as physiological differences (the parent is in the process of losing his full powers at the same time that the child is beginning to acquire his), psychosocial differences ("adult realism versus youthful idealism"), and sociological differences (status differentials between the young and the old). These explanations may suggest ways to reconcile the differences between the maturational model and the experiential model.

In recent years social scientists have to some degree addressed these three models in their explorations of political change. Jennings and Niemi (1975) conducted a paired panel study of parents and their adolescent children in an attempt to test several plausible generational hypotheses. They found that in the United States there has been a convergence of these two generations due both to life cycle effects among the young as well as to changes in the attitudes of the adults that brought them closer to their children. Lipset and Ladd (1972) examined the same generation of American youth and concurred that their data seemed to support the life cycle model of value change.

Others, however, have concluded that the experiential model is more accurate. Sociologists Glenn and Hefner (1972) argue that their data fail to support the maturation thesis because American generations do not seem to have become more conservative over time. Abramson (1976), through the use of time series survey data, argues that the decline in party identification in the United States is a function of experientially formed generational differences, and not a reflection of the life cycle model of party identification suggested by Campbell et al. (1960). In a longitudinal study of the careers and political orientations of radical students in Japan, Krauss (1974) demonstrated support for the experiential explanation, especially among the most highly politicized in his sample. Bauer et al. (1961) also employ the experiential model in explorations of political change in the Soviet Union. Ike (1973), in his examination of Japanese survey data, suggests that more than one variety of generational change obtains.

Fewer studies have been explicitly directed at the examination of generational change in the context of the interaction model. One such study was completed in which the interaction hypothesis was explained for a sample of Indian youths and their families (Sinda and Gangrade 1969). Feuer (1972)

---

[a]Lane (1959) argues that contrary to Davis' thesis, American culture discourages parent-child conflict.

compares the Russian, French, and American revolutionary movements and analyzes the generational component in each. He emphasizes the ways in which the conflict of young versus old was superimposed upon class and other factors in the Russian Revolution.

By his treatment of all three models, Huntington sets the framework for the subsequent contributions to this volume. His analyses are utilized both implicitly and explicitly as recurring themes in the more area-specific presentations. Each of the contributors to this volume was concerned not only with the analysis of the particular type of generational configuration that obtained in their country or region, but also with the ways in which *any* sort of generational explanation contributed to the understanding of politics. Each was concerned with the utility of the generational concept vis-à-vis other formulations of social and political cleavage. Political generations are, as Mannheim (1928) first suggested, only one sort of "social location" (p. 291). There are many others such as class, ethnicity, and religion that have relevance for political study. Yet the concept of political generations offers the investigator an advantage in some polities, for it is potentially cross-stratal—that is, where class or ethnicity or religion or other such "social locations" do not preselect individuals' experiences. In this context Harold Isaacs finds the concept useful. Similarly, Alfred Stepan and Amos Perlmutter, in exploring political change in Latin America and Israel respectively, suggest that the generational idea, when understood in the context of an institutional nexus (the military, the party apparatus), offers the researcher a useful framework within which he can come to grips with political change, although both also suggest qualifications of the generational concept.

Several other contributors also note the need to qualify the generational concept. Lucian Pye argues that while there are at least four sharply layered generations in China, each differentiated from the next by its date of entry into the party apparatus, they are also cross-cut by three functional clusters within the Chinese polity. Moreover, Pye suggests that these four generations hold less significance as a group than does the single most important generation, the gerontocratic elite of the Long March that has controlled the nation since 1949. William Quandt also offers qualifications of the generational argument as it is applied to the Arab world. He argues that generations are more appropriate as foci of study in some Arab nations than in others. Its utility is tempered by such factors as the character of prior nationalist struggles, the history of tribalism, and the nature of monarchical regimes.

Martin Kilson rejects the generational concept in its application to black Americans. The other contributors to this collection focus upon elite generations, but Kilson's analysis is concerned with attitude change at the mass level. Here again, Mannheim's (1928) seminal essay serves to inform our inquiry. Mannheim sees generations as agents of cultural change. They often serve to shape "the spirit of the age" (*Zeitgeist*), and in doing so their orientations may come to be sharply discontinuous with those of prior generations. This idea of sharp discontinuity is what Kilson employs as a measure of the generational component in the process of social change among blacks in the United States. He sees continuity, not marked differentiation, across age cohorts of Afro-Americans when institutional affiliation is accounted for. He thus contests the utility of the generational approach in the study of black Americans.

The discussion of political generations among elites inevitably implies also the process of succession to power. This connection is made explicit in the presentations by Lucian Pye and William Griffith. Griffith addresses generational change among elites in the Soviet Union and Eastern Europe, and in so doing he identifies the bureaucratic gerontocracies that have come to govern these politics. He does not deny that there is generational mobility, but he attributes such mobility to such cataclysmic events as the Stalinist purges. Regularized channels of succession to power do not appear to have been forged in these political systems. Pye is also concerned with the nature of gerontocratic rule, but he suggests that in the case of China the succession problem is one of individual and not institutional legitimacy. Pye discusses Mao Tse-tung as the charismatic figure, as the great leader who is at the same time both the inspiration for Chinese politics as well as the impediment to political succession. He argues that beneath the charisma of Mao is an underlying narcissism that prevents him from maintaining an enduring commitment to the heirs of his power. Mao has abandoned his personally chosen successors, each in turn, and in doing so he has enhanced conditions favorable to generational conflict.

Sigmund Neumann (1939), in describing World War I as a watershed separating political generations in Europe, speaks of the gerontocracies that had marked European leadership at the end of the conflict: "The generation of young fighters became a tragic generation of outsiders" (p. 625). The theme of excluded counterelites is also found in the presentations by Harold Isaacs and Alfred Stepan in this volume. Stepan is concerned with describing the different ways in which formerly excluded military cohorts interpret their political roles in Peru and Brazil. Isaacs' is a more comprehensive treatment of the differences between the nationalist generation of Third World leaders and the postcolonial generation. This latter group was the first generation to have to confront the realities and imperatives presented by underdevelopment. He tells the story of the ways in which the purity of nationalist ideals was transformed (and in many cases compromised) by the demands of political order. This is very much a generational story of political succession in the new states.

Political order and generational succession are also themes in the contributions to this collection made by Myron Weiner and Amos Perlmutter. Both are concerned with the authoritarian political apparatus of the dominant political party in a new state. Perlmutter describes the founding fathers of the modern Israeli state as divided between ideologists and apparatchiks. Together they comprise what he labels the Bolshevik generation in Israel. The successor to this generation in Israel is comprised quite literally of the children of the apparatchiks.

6

He concludes that while generations are clearly identifiable, there does not appear to be significant generational change. Weiner addresses the case of India, one of the most vivid examples of familial succession outside of a monarchy. He details institutional change in India and the role played in this process by the personal leadership of four generations in the same lineage. This presentation was made at most perplexing time in Indian history; the "National Emergency" was not yet one year old, and both Indira Gandhi and her son Sanjay were in the process of consolidating unprecedented power on the subcontinent.

The critical reader will be aware that in none of these contributions is the concept of generational cohorts offered as a substitute for other forms of politically relevant groups. We must ask: Where do generational models seem to have the greatest utility? Where are they most vivid? Under what conditions do the models best apply? We will remember Mannheim's (1928) conviction that the rapidity with which new generations are introduced into the political process depends upon the rate and character of change in a given polity. His hypothesis is straightforward, and it is rooted in his model of generations as experientially formed. As change accelerates there is an accompanying acceleration of potentially socializing events; hence there is an increase in the number of politically significant generational groups. If this is valid then we can expect to find among the presentations to this volume evidence that the experiential model is more applicable to revolutionary societies, those with genuine discontinuities, than to established systems. In these latter systems we might expect the maturation thesis to have greater relevance. We should also find that peoples who have experienced nationalist struggles are more inclined to be divided by generations than are peoples who have not. This may no doubt be related to the accelerated rate with which newly politicized participants enter the political process. We should also find that the rise of newly powerful institutions such as political parties and military units encourage the formation of political generations by delimiting their membership's political experiences.

The answers that we find are not so pat, indeed our answers seldom are. But this volume offers an assessment of the generational concept in a wide variety of political systems. It should suggest to the reader that generational change and political development are often associated in nontrivial ways. Further, it should also suggest the need for additional scholarship concerning their relationship.

References

Abramson, Paul R. 1976. "Generational Change and the Decline of Party Identification in America: 1952-1974." *American Political Science Review*, vol. 70, no. 2 (June), pp. 469-78.

Ashford, Douglas E. 1963. *Second and Third Generation Elites in the Maghreb.* Washington, D.C.: U.S. Department of State.

7

Bauer, Raymond A., et al. 1961. *How the Soviet System Works: Cultural, Psychological and Social Themes*. New York: Vintage Books.

Berger, Bennett M. 1960. "How Long is a Generation?" *The British Journal of Sociology*, vol. 11, no. 1 (March), pp. 10–23.

Butler, David, and Stokes, Donald. 1971. *Political Change in Britain*. New York: St. Martins.

Campbell, Angus, et al. 1960. *The American Voter*. New York: Wiley.

Davis, Kingsley. 1940. "The Sociology of Parent-Youth Conflict." *American Sociological Review*, vol. 5, no. 4 (August), pp. 523–35.

Eisenstadt, S.N. 1956. *From Generation to Generation: Age Groups and Social Structure*. Glencoe, Ill.: Free Press.

Feuer, Lewis S. 1972. "Generations and the Theory of Revolution." *Survey*, vol. 18, no. 3 (Summer), pp. 161–88.

Glenn, N.D., and Hefner, T. 1972. "Further Evidence on Aging and Party Identification." *Public Opinion Quarterly*, vol. 36, no. 1 (Spring), pp. 31–47.

Goertzel, Ted. 1972. "Generational Conflict and Social Change." *Youth and Society*, vol. 3, no. 3 (March), pp. 327–52.

Gusfield, Joseph R. 1957. "The Problems of Generations in an Organizational Structure." *Social Forces*, vol. 35, no. 4 (May), pp. 323–30.

Heberle, Rudolf. 1951. *Social Movements: An Introduction to Political Sociology*. New York: Appelton.

Ike, Nobutaka. 1973. "Economic Growth and Intergenerational Change in Japan," *American Political Science Review*, vol. 67, no. 4 (December), pp. 1194–203.

Inglehart, Ronald. 1971. "The Silent Revolution in Europe: Intergenerational Change in Post-Industrial Societies." *American Political Science Review*, vol. 65, no. 4 (December), pp. 991–1017.

Jennings, M. Kent, and Niemi, Richard G. 1975. "Continuity and Change in Political Orientations: A Longitudinal Study of Two Generations." *American Political Science Review*, vol. 69, no. 4 (December), pp. 1316–35.

Krauss, Ellis S. 1974. *Japanese Radicals Revisited: Student Protest in Postwar Japan*. Berkeley: University of California Press.

Lane, Robert E. 1959. "Fathers and Sons: Foundations of Political Beliefs." *American Sociological Review*, vol. 24, no. 4 (August), pp. 502–11.

Linton, Ralph. 1942. "Age and Sex Categories." *American Sociological Review*, vol. 7, no. 5 (October), pp. 589–603.

Lipset, S.M., and Ladd, E.C., Jr. 1972. "The Political Future of Activist Generations," pp. 63–84. In Philip G. Altbach and Robert S. Laufer (eds.), *The New Pilgrims: Youth Protest in Transition*. New York: David McKay.

Mannheim, Karl. 1928, 1952. *Essays on the Sociology of Knowledge*. London: Routledge and Kegan Paul.

Neumann, Sigmund. 1939. "The Conflict of Generations in Contemporary Europe from Versailles to Munich." *Vital Speeches of the Day*, vol. 5, pp. 623-628.

———. 1965. *Permanent Revolution: Totalitarianism in the Age of International Civil War*, 2nd ed. New York: Praeger.

Quandt, William. 1969. *Revolution and Political Leadership: Algeria 1954-1968.* Cambridge, Mass.: MIT Press.

Riley, Matilda White. 1973. "Aging and Cohort Succession: Interpretations and Misinterpretations." *Public Opinion Quarterly*, vol. 37, no. 1 (Spring), pp. 35-49.

Rintala, Marvin. 1968. "Political Generations," pp. 92-96. in David L. Sills (ed.), *International Encyclopedia of the Social Sciences*, Vol. 6. New York: The Macmillan Company and The Free Press.

Sinha, M.P., and Gangrade, K.D. (eds.). 1971. *Inter-Generational Conflict in India*. Bombay: Nachiketa Publications.

2

Generations, Cycles, and Their Role in American Development

Samuel P. Huntington

One way to distinguish one generation from another is the relative amount of interest that each generation manifests in the idea of generations itself. The extent to which scholars and social theorists focus on generations as a problem, or the extent to which they find the concept useful, may help in defining a generation. Historically, we find that this changes often. The first major theorist of generations was Plato, and the idea was a popular one in fourth century B.C. Greece. Generations and the closely related concept of cycles also manifested themselves in Roman thought. More recently, there was a major recurrence of interest among Western social theorists in the years after World War I. And now again in the past six years there seems to be a return to the concept of generations. This record immediately suggests one conceivable generalization concerning generations: People turn to the idea of generations and find it useful during or immediately after a time of troubles, social trauma, and upheaval. This was certainly true in the case of Plato; it was certainly true in the cases of Neumann, Mannheim, and Sorokin in the 1920s and 1930s; and it may well be true today, as people perceive that we are in a time of troubles and major discontinuity.

During the last half dozen years or so there has been something less than a flood, yet something more than a trickle of studies concerning the idea of generations. A number of these, focusing on the United States, have used survey data to analyze generational factors in opinion and voting. There has been a reopening of the debate between the life cycle (maturation) theory, on the one hand, and the experiential emphasis, on the other. There has also been a smaller body of literature looking at the relationship of generational concepts and experiences to attitudes on foreign policy. Thus, the idea of generations seems to be coming back into use. This may or may not be a good thing.

The Concept of Generations

One of the problems in dealing with generations is, of course, the nature of the concept itself. It can mean a variety of things. There is a great danger in judging virtually everything in terms of generations or generational differences. When we talk about generations with respect to politics, it seems to me that we are talking about one or more of three things. As a minimal definition, we talk about an age cohort, defined in terms of time of birth, whose members may

9

share certain attitudes and behavioral patterns. Here one can speak of the New Deal generation, for example. This is a group that matured in the early 1930s and has a distinctive pattern of voting. Survey data show that quite clearly. A second-level definition would look at an age cohort in which the members *conceive* of themselves as being distinctive; not only do they share particular political characteristics, but there is a consciousness as well. This definition is not unlike the concept of class consciousness. We can see this idea of conciousness in a variety of settings, but perhaps we see it most often when the older are talking about the younger, when there is a consciousness of "us" versus "them." Thirdly, and in the fullest sense, we can conceive of a generation not only as an age cohort in which members share certain political characteristics and in which they have a consciousness of themselves as a group, but in addition, where there is an interaction among the members—that is, where there is interaction for the purpose of achieving political results. We might cite the Venezuelan example of the "generation of '28," which refers to a group of political leaders who emerged from the University in 1928 to found the Accion Democratica. This group included people like Betancourt and Lenoni who controlled that party and held power in Venezuela for some thirty years from the late 1930s to the mid-1960s. This is a generation in the third, and fullest, sense of the word.

As noted earlier, we can think of a generation as being somewhat like a class. It is very hard to draw a line to distinguish one generation from another, just as it is difficult to distinguish one class from another. In one sense, when we think about generations we are stratifying people by age, just as we are stratifying people by wealth or income when we conceptualize classes. There is a difficulty in carrying this analogy very far, however, in that a generation, unlike a class, is a transitory phenomenon. In the extended analogy we would have to envision total class mobility; the "classes"—that is, the generations, are not standing still, but are continually changing.

The problem gets more confused because there is a tendency to be relatively loose in the use of the concept of generations. I think it is necessary to distinguish the phenomenon of generations from the simple passage of time. It is quite clear that the generation of leaders in the United States in the 1940s was concerned with the war against Hitler. The generation of leaders in the 1960s was concerned with the war on poverty, among other things. To say that these differences represent a generational change, however, is stretching the concept too far. It is hardly surprising that two different groups of people do two different things at two different points in time. This would be more a function of history than of generational differences. What we should be interested in doing when we analyze politics in terms of generations is not elaborating that point, but looking at a situation in which there are two different generations doing two different things at the *same* point in time. When the generational factor manifests itself in a cleavage at a single time, rather than in a shift from one time to another, the concept really becomes interesting.

Explaining Generational Differences

I can suggest three theories to explain generational activity and generational differences (Table 2-1). One theory, that of the *life cycle* or *maturation* approach, suggests that the significant difference is one of age. This implies that as the young get older, they will become like what the older were previously. The cohort changes, but there is not much change in the society. This view corresponds to the image of a stable society in which generational conflict is continuous; there will always be young, there always will be old, and they will always be distinguishable by a certain number of years. But the conflict will always be moderate because both parties are continuously changing; the young age, and the aged die.

Sidney Verba and Norman Nie (1972), in their book *Participation in America*, have a chapter on age in which they look at the argument that political participation follows a curvilinear pattern in which the young and the old are not as participant as those in the middle years of life. They come up with some very interesting data that suggest that this is not the case. In fact, once one controls for socioeconomic status, there tends to be a strong *linear* correlation between age and participation. The young don't participate as much as the middle-aged, and the more elderly tend to participate more than both (although there is a slight dropoff among the most elderly). This, then, would imply that voting propensity is a function of one's position in the life cycle.

A second way of explaining generational differences is what can be called the *interaction* theory. It ties in with some cyclical theories, which will be mentioned a bit later. In the interaction model, one generation is seen as reacting against another, which would mean that the differences between generations are the product of sequence. Change does take place in the society, and conflict will be brief but will recur with each new generation to a fairly intense degree.

Table 2-1
Theories Explaining Generational Differences

Theory	Differences Function of	Compared to Predecessor Each New Cohort is	Change Takes Place in	Generational Conflict	
				Time	Degree
Maturation (life cycle)	Age	Similar	Cohort	Continuous	Moderate
Interaction	Sequence	Different	Society	Brief Recurring	Intense
Experiential	Experience	Similar/ Different	Society	Brief Irregular	Intense

The interaction model was articulated explicitly and in considerable detail by Plato, who, as you will remember, in *The Republic* analyzed the decay of the ideal state in terms of the reaction of one generation against the values and goals of the preceding generation. John Adams once suggested a somewhat similar pattern of change among generations, and in the 1960s Walt Rostow discussed what he termed, after Thomas Mann, "the Buddenbrooks dynamics," to describe the changing perspectives of generations in the course of economic development.

The third theory can be called the *experiential* theory; it has received the most attention in recent years. In this case, the most decisive factor in generational formation is the shared experience of an age cohort. The focus is usually on what happens to a particular cohort when it is at its most formative age. Studies have focused on the role of World War I in forming political generations in Europe. Others have focused on the impact of the Depression and the New Deal on voting and have challenged the hypotheses of the life cycle model that attitudes of liberal-conservatism in the United States vary directly with age. To the contrary, data for the 1950s show that those who came of age in the United States in the 1920s were relatively conservative; those who came of age in the 1930s were relatively liberal; and those who came of age in the late 1940s were relatively conservative again. Quite clearly, here the experiential theory is a better explanation than is the maturation theory. In more general terms, one useful thing about the experiential theory is that it allows for both variations in the intensity of generational conflict and for the *degree* of generational difference. There may thus be significant variation over time in the degree to which the generational model is relevant. Here, some data from the Michigan Survey Research Center is useful (Table 2-2).

As we can see from Table 2-2, the variation among age groups in 1952 is not significant. There is a somewhat greater differentiation among age groups in 1960, and by 1968 there is a substantial difference between the youngest age group and the oldest one. It should also be pointed out that there is a clear shift in the opinion of all groups on this particular question over the sixteen-year period. The oldest age group in 1968, those born between 1900 and 1907, shifted their opinion from 82 percent agreement to 62 percent agreement between 1952 and 1968. What is even more striking, it seems to me, is the way in which the difference between generations opened up. Both the shift in terms of the differences across time of the same age cohort and the differences that are opened up between the younger and older age groups can be explained, presumably by some experience that occurred in the late 1950s and intensified in the 1960s. We could do the same kind of analysis with foreign policy issues. In 1952 I would suspect that there would not be a great deal of difference among age groups on foreign policy questions. By 1968, I am sure that we would find quite substantial differences between generations. On this point the work of Graham Allison (1970-71) is instructive.

Table 2-2
Age and Attitudes Toward Voting

Percentage agreeing with the statement, "Voting is the only way that people like me can have any say about how the government runs things."

	Election Year (age in parentheses)		
Year of Birth	1952	1960	1968
1940–1947			37% (21–28)
1932–1939		69% (21–28)	41% (29–36)
1924–1931	79% (21–28)	69% (29–36)	44% (37–44)
1916–1923	74% (29–36)	67% (37–44)	49% (45–52)
1908–1915	81% (37–44)	74% (45–52)	56% (53–60)
1900–1907	82% (45–52)	74% (53–60)	62% (61+)
1892–1899	84% (53–60)	78% (61+)	
Before 1892	80% (61+)		
Difference between oldest and youngest strata	+1	+9	+25
Total electorate	80%	72%	49%
Total sample	1,899	1,954	1,557

Source: Anne Foner, "Age Stratification and Age Conflict in Political Life," *American Sociological Review*, vol. 39 (April 1974). Reprinted with permission.

Generations in American Politics

There is also the question of whether generations have peculiar relevance to the study of American politics. I have not seen any test of the hypothesis that generational differences are more significant in the United States than in other societies. If in fact there is not any data available at the moment supporting this proposition, there are at least four good reasons why there should be. First of all, a generational analysis should be particularly relevant to "founded" societies—that is, those societies that have a distinct beginning in time. The United States, in a sense, has been founded not once, but twice. Once in the sense that there was a process of settlement and immigration that represents a distinct starting point. We can thus speak of the Massachusetts Bay Colony in terms of first, second, and third generations. We can and do speak of immigrant groups in the same manner. One can also look at the U.S. case in terms of the generational sequence that starts with the national founding and the revolutionary generation. At least in the early history of founded societies the differences in generations may be significant. We can look at the differences between the American revolutionary generation, the generation of the War of 1812, and the Jacksonian generation as reasonably discrete groups that suggest evidence of generational differences and conflict.

A second reason why generations ought to be more important in the case of the United States than elsewhere is because the United States is to some degree a consensual society. With the blurring of class lines, other types of distinctions should be more important. Moreover, we've had a *moving* consensus due to rapid change; this consensus is redefined by each generation. Consequently, there is conflict over the nature of this redefinition of American ideals and goals in each generation. This also helps explain why conflict in America has such a fleeting quality.

Thirdly, the United States has been, in comparison to other societies, an extremely democratic and egalitarian society. As far as politics is concerned, this means that political struggle is quite likely to be more on a generational basis. In a society with vertical lines of authority, people will try to get ahead by finding a patron to ensure their success. This pattern can be contrasted to the peer group model, which is more relevant to the American case. The patron-client model obviously applies to bureaucratic structures such as corporations and universities, but American electoral politics has not worked that way. Instead, the peer group model applies. When incumbents are defeated, there is very often a substantial age difference between those who come in and those who go out. This difference suggests an easily testable hypothesis: There should be a greater spread in ages between an incumbent candidate and his followers and a nonincumbent candidate and his followers in the United States than in other societies.

A fourth reason why generations may be particularly relevant to the United States concerns the extent to which rapid social change can define new generations very quickly, in experiential terms. The number of politically relevant generations is multiplied by the nature of a rapidly changing society. The whole question of how many generations there are at any one time is an important one, and it is in part a function of how many different experiences there are that allow age-cohorts to think of themselves as being different from each other.

Political Cycles and Generations

Let me conclude with a brief note on the question of cycles. I think we can relate cycles to generational analyses. They clearly are not identical; we can think of cycles that are not generational and of generational cleavages that have nothing to do with cycles. But particularly if we speak of the interaction pattern, there are some developments among generations that may occur in cyclical terms. Again, I don't know if there is any systematic basis for this, but there certainly is an extraordinary tendency to interpret American politics in terms of cycles. Table 2-3 summarizes four of the most familiar cyclical interpretations. Some of the reasons

Table 2-3
Some Cyclical Theories of American Politics

Liberalism and Conservatism[a]

Liberal	Conservative
1765–1787	1787–1801
1801–1816	1816–1829
1829–1841	1841–1861
1861–1869	1869–1901
1901–1919	1919–1931
1931–1947	

Party Realignment and Critical Elections[b]

1789–1800	1860–1896
1800–1828	1896–1932
1828–1860	1932–

Introversion and Extroversion[c]

Introversion	Extroversion
1776–1798	1798–1824
1824–1844	1844–1871
1871–1891	1891–1919
1919–1940	1940–

Mobility Cycles for Governmental Leadership[d]

Birth cohorts in which high percentages of governmental leaders came from fairly ordinary homes.

1745–1747	1835–1837
1769–1771	1856–1858
1787–1789	1874–1876
1811–1813	

Sources:

[a]Arthur M. Schlesinger, *Paths to the Present* (Boston: Houghton Mifflin, 1964), pp. 92–93.

[b]Walter Dean Burnham, *Critical Elections and the Mainsprings of American Politics* (New York: W.W. Norton, 1970); Arthur Holcombe, *The Political Parties of Today: A Study in Republican and Democratic Politics* (New York: Harper Brothers, 1924), ch. 12; V.O. Key Jr., "A Theory of Critical Elections," *Journal of Politics*, Vol. XVII (1955); Charles G. Sellers, "The Equilibrium Cycle in Two-Party Politics," *Public Opinion Quarterly*, vol. XXX (1965).

[c]Frank L. Klingberg, "The Historical Alteration of Moods in American Foreign Policy," *"World Politics*, vol. IV (January 1952), pp. 239–73.

[d]P.M.G. Harris, "The Social Origins of American Leaders: The Demographic Foundations," *Perspectives in American History*, vol. III (1969), pp. 159–346.

for these theories might be the same reasons why generational theories may be seen as relevant to American politics. This phenomenon is worthy of more extensive analysis. I should add that there may be a tendency for political scientists to ignore, or not give due weight to, the role of cycles in politics. We're used to thinking about *economic* cycles, but we're not really used to thinking about *political* cycles. There is a tendency to view cyclical interpretations as being somehow mechanistic, rather primitive, and unsophisticated. We can, however, develop quite sophisticated psychological reasons as to why certain patterns of behavior might well recur in a cyclical pattern.

Discussion

Weiner:

In talking about the conditions under which generational models are salient as opposed to models of class or ethnicity, you suggested that several were at work in the United States. You spoke of founded societies, consensual societies, democratic and egalitarian societies, and societies of rapid social change. The other side of the argument would posit older societies, highly conflictual societies, hierarchial or authoritarian societies, and those with slow rates of social change. These factors then, would presumably obstruct the salience of generational explanations. I think your argument would then be that to the extent that some developing nations are in this latter group of categories, you would find other explanations of politics more useful than generational ones.

Dominquez:

One comment that you made in your remarks concerned the fairly sharp distinction between the United States and Western Europe in terms of the applicability of generational analysis. I'm not sure I agree with that. I think there is some data, supplied by Inglehart, that uncover some degree of difference between the United States and Western Europe but do not suggest the dichotomy that you seem to indicate. There have been several other papers, one is by Marsh in the *APSR* (1975), that argue that generations do exist and that they do have a systematic impact on social class. It is not your saying that generations are not relevant in other industrial societies, but it is a matter of your stressing a dichotomy more than a mere difference in patterns.

All of the articles that I can think of in this context address this issue in the post-World War II context. They try to stress the increasing weight of generational factors in contrast to other factors. So one could say that the issue becomes why do Western European countries and Japan become more similar to the United States in terms of the importance of generations since World War II? From this one could infer the End of Ideology argument—that is, there are a number of characteristics and factors common to industrial societies that have reduced the conflict based on social class and that have increased the weight of conflict based on the experiential generational model.

Verba:

On this same point, there could be added another possible variable. One of the things that seemed to be missing from your list as to why generational differences appear greater in the United States had to do with the organizational characteristics of youth in the United States. Just as the workers were able to organize when they all came together in factories, a characteristic of American youth is that they are kept off the street longer than others by being in universities for an extended period of time. Much of the generation gap does not appear to be something that characterizes the full range of youth, but just that part of youth that is on university campuses. And that of course is a major difference between the United States and most other societies; the United States has a very high proportion of youth who fall into that category. This is not inconsistent with what Jorge Dominquez was saying about the European case. Much of those kinds of postindustrial values tend to be those exemplified by university students across the world. The key is the particular structure in which people are held together in ways in which they can organize, communicate, and form a class.

von Pfetten:

In Germany over the last two hundred years we've had the largest number of political upheavals in Europe. The majority of those can be quite clearly attributed to generational changes. A typical case is the post-Bismarck period when the young and inexperienced Kaiser said that he couldn't play as the old man himself could with seven balls at one time. Or we could turn to the late 1960s in Paris at a time of great student unrest. The bringing down of the Gaullist regime had clear generational overtones. The same thing happened, perhaps even more clearly, in Germany, where a generation that was conscious of having lived through the war is being followed by a generation without that experience. Yet for all of the evidence of generational factors in Europe, none of your four points really apply. Yet you could explain a very large amount of social and political change in Germany by generational theories.

Huntington:

I would agree with most of what you have to say, but I think that there is a problem of interpreting everything in terms of generational factors. The fact that the young Kaiser couldn't do what Bismark did is probably more a function of the difference between the Kaiser and Bismark than of their difference in age.

Haviland:

I think that we're all agreed that generational differences is one of the bases of conflict and differentiation. But we have to remind ourselves that there are many such bases. Perhaps this is a good corrective to the class emphases and to others that attempt to exclude other factors. There are a myriad of cleavages—tribal, nationalistic, and so forth.

We also have to consider what is happening in a society that creates these generational differences. The main thing perhaps is not to speak of generational differences, but to understand what *makes* them different.

The third point I would make is that we also must remind ourselves of the salient differences *within* generations. Within each generation there are often as many important differences as there are between generations. You still have the rich versus the poor, regional differences, religious differences, and language differences. I don't think that we've escaped any of the complexities of human conflict.

Huntington:

As a footnote to that, one thing which may differ from one generation to another is the significance of those other differences within generations that you mentioned. There is evidence that suggests that the generation that came of age in the United States during the New Deal is much more split along class lines than either the generation that preceded it or the one that followed it.

Field:

Does the experiential model allow for nondirect, derived exposure? In other words, what of the *sons* of those who went through the Depression, and what of the *sons* of the Cold War generation? These are persons who have in many cases imbibed the values of their parents.

I was born in 1940, my parents lived through the Depression, which was the most important formative political experience of their lives. It changed them from Republicans to Democrats. I'm a Democrat. My perception of issues in American politics is derived from the Depression and from the cleavages that arose in that context.

So, in terms of your model, I can't place myself in the maturation theory, I can't place myself in the interaction theory, and I can't place myself in the experiential theory. I find myself in the category of *derived* experience.

Huntington:

Presumably you would have a certain congruence within the age cohort of the offspring of the New Deal generation. Your experience is one that could be generalized to others who were born in the early 1940s.

There is some work done by Stanley Rothman that looks at the radicalism of the youth of the 1960s and explores it as a consequence of their being the children of those who were radical in the 1930s. The children were radical because of their parents' experience, and this could be interpreted as a derived experiential pattern.

Schneider:

There is evidence that people at a certain age are particularly susceptible to bias in the political and informational environment, the age at which they first enter the electorate. These kinds of generational changes do not portend generational conflict. The New Deal generation and the "silent" generation of the 1950s have distinctive outlines that may have nothing to do with generational conflict. On the other hand, the generation of the 1960s in the United States was firmly impressed by a conflict in which the two sides of the issue were polarized on values and policy. That polarization was more than anything else a generational difference. One could argue that since the mid-1960s, when the most important issue was Civil Rights, liberalism on Civil Rights continues to be quite prominent among younger generations of Americans. It was a kind of *Zeitgeist*. But the Vietnam War was different in that it was an issue that polarized the younger and older generations. Perhaps this would fit the interaction model.

As far as extending this to Western Europe, it is my impression that one has generations that do differ in the way that Inglehart describes. What they have not yet found is their Vietnam. There is the search for a political issue on which they can really close ranks. So the question is, does this fit the experiential or the interaction model?

Huntington:

I think that this would probably fall under the experiential model. The Vietnam War is something that the young experienced in the 1960s and the argument has been made that the experience of Munich and Pearl Harbor sets the framework for the older generation. If it had been a question of interaction, you would have predicted that while the Munich-Pearl Harbor generation drew certain conclusions, the 1950s generation would have reacted against that and drawn different conclusions.

What happened instead was the impact of another experience—Vietnam. It was that experience, rather than the older generation, that people were really reacting to.

Schneider:

Let me introduce a new distinction, then. My reading of the Vietnam event was that it was one where the major cleavage was generational. So, if one takes any point in time, the conflict is very much across generations. That was probably not true of the Depression or of the Civil Rights issues of the early 1960s. Those cases were experiential, but were not cases where at any given point in time the conflict was between generations.

Huntington:

Let's remember the three dimensions we have for looking at generations. First, there is the difference between one age cohort and another in terms of political values, attitudes, and so forth. Second, there is the question of whether the age cohort thinks of itself as a generation—that is, whether it is self-conscious. Third is the dimension that concerns conflict between the generations. You can certainly have differences without conflict. What you are saying is that in these earlier periods there were differences, but not conflict.

The experiential model is tied in with the socialization process, but there is an earlier, large body of literature on attitude formation that stressed the significance of the very early years from ages three to thirteen. In effect, what this experiential model emphasizes is a later phase in the life cycle where events *overcome* whatever previous socialization had occurred.

The question of what kind of theory exists to explain cycles and inter-action is an important issue. I would think one would look for an answer in the psychological literature. If one is to make cyclical theories persuasive, one would certainly have to do this. Psychological explanations have been offered for the phenomenon of the business cycle and for price fluctuations. It involves the rejection of rational choice models of human behavior. I think that one can certainly come up with psychological theories that can undergird interaction or cyclical models.

Migdal:

The experiential model is very substance oriented—that is, we are forced to look at structural phenomena. The interaction model is not. It merely says this is the way man is. Therefore, we're not going to find very much variability here. The nice thing about Marx's dialectics is that they tell us that A begets B and that B is going to be destructive toward A. The psychological theories that I've seen do not really do that, and thus they don't allow us to deal with cases in which children *don't* react against their parents.

Verba:

I think that there is one problem that we should try to get straight in this whole notion of generations and cyclical models. It seems to make sense if you talk about an individual family. There are the Rockefellers and then thirty years later there are the junior Rockefellers. If you think about a society as a whole, things don't happen in thirty-year periods. One age group is constantly replacing another age group, and there is nothing in that flow of replacements that can explain sharp discontinuities. In general, the cyclical models just don't seem to explain as much as do historical models, because new generations appear constantly, not just every thirty years.

Bill Schneider made the point concerning the relationship between the transmission of values in the family and these sudden historical discontinuities. They can be nicely illustrated if we go back to the reason why John Field became a Democrat. He is absolutely archetypical in that respect. It is a good example of the interaction between family transmission of values and historical events. He came of age in the late 1950s, and his parents became Democrats in the New Deal Era. He inherited this affiliation in the late 1950s, although in the late 1960s he wouldn't have. The main point is that the generation that came of age in the late 1950s came of age after the party realignment of the 1930s had been finished and frozen, based on the issues of the 1930s. They no longer believed in those issues, but there were no other issues around. So they basically inherited the party affiliation of their parents—that is, the children of Democrats became Democrats; by the late 1960s, the number was down to under 50 percent. In a late era, children grow up with the same set of parents, but there is a new force that, while not pushing them into the other political party, pushes them *away* from parties altogether. It is at times when there are no alternative forces operating that you get a very high level of stable transmission.

Huntington:

That is really purely experiential. What you are saying is that the experience of one generation is transmitted to a succeeding generation in the absence of any other dramatic experience.

Pool:

The outlining of the differences in these theories I find extremely clear, enlightening, and persuasive. So much so that if I were a man from Mars who had come down and heard this discussion, I would have been severely misled. I would have been convinced that the generational concept is a very important and effective dynamic of politics; that we ought to be able to observe generational differences just by the most casual look at the political process; that we ought to be able to categorize people by the generation that they belong to. But it isn't that way at all. The thing that really needs explaining is why, given all these mechanisms, the generational results are so obscure. Here is a group of political scientists that has succeeded in determining that there *are* generations and generational effects. This is almost a discovery.

This needs explaining. All the mechanisms that you've talked about are there. There is the maturation process, there is reaction, and there is the experiential elements. Why then is it all so invisible twenty years later? We're not speaking of youth politics, which is a different matter. In speaking of generational politics we should be talking about lasting effects. I think that there are a number of reasons, many of which you've identified. They are all happening, but they don't converge in their impact. You may have a maturation effect simultaneous to an experiential effect, and moving in opposite directions. I agree with Sid Verba that it is also due to the fact that generations don't come neatly packaged in the way that elections do, every four or every thirty years. A difference of two or three years might constitute a generational difference among college-aged youth, but not among the middle-aged.

Also, twenty or thirty years later the issues are different. So, you've got a generation that knows that the answer is Munich, but history presents a new set of events for which the answers are not pat. Then, too, there is the fact that twenty years later, this generation has gone through a whole set of additional experiences. So what we're talking about is a series of processes that are there, and that you've outlined very nicely, but perhaps the impressive fact is that they make so little an impact on politics.

Huntington:

I think that there is something to what you say. As I suggested at the outset of my remarks, the perception of generations changes from time to time, and indeed the importance of generations changes from time to time. In the 1950s, generational differences weren't very important. They became important in the 1960s. Changes in the significance of the generational factor may also be accompanied by changes in the perception of it. We've gone through periods in social science of rediscovering classes and ethnicity, and now generations are back.

Bennett:

I'm perfectly content with any sort of noneconomic explanations like those of race, region, religion, or generation. But what bothers me is that once you've accepted this generational approach, it becomes salient to only a small range of issues. The ones that have been raised here have been the same ones over and over again: World War II, the Depression, and Vietnam. I think that this is really Ithiel Pool's point. The differences in the generations are so obvious, and the political manifestations of these generational differences are so hard to find. If you are offering this as an alternative to class explanations, you would have to be able to explain how you can explain the kinds of economic differences and economic attitudes that you can explain by class by means of a generational model.

Huntington:

Let me repeat: I certainly wouldn't argue that you should try to explain every-thing in generational terms. I'm not saying that all history is the history of generational struggle. The interesting question is what roles do generational differences play in comparison to class, ethnic, or various other potential lines of cleavage. I do think, however, that generational differences have been signi-ficant in the survey data that has been available and that there is evidence for the salience of generations in other contexts as well. For example, Lawrence Stone, (1972), in his book on the causes of the English Revolution, makes the point that in 1640 in the British Parliament there was a very marked generational distinction. Those MP's who were over fifty were two-to-one on the side of the roundheads; those MP's who were under fifty were two-to-one on the side of the King. There is also a study of Cuba that shows that in terms of the attitudes toward the Castro revolution the younger generation was less favorably disposed toward the revolution than was the older generation.

Elliot:

One thing that the generational model continues to return to, although we deny it, is the question of what happens to young people upon entering politics. That seems to be the strongest place where it comes forward. I wonder if we couldn't cut it another way and say that what we're really looking at is the question of new entrants into politics. Then we've got young people as one group of new entrants, we've got immigrants as another, and we've got women, blacks, and other previously excluded political actors. What we see in each of these groups of new entrants is that the ages get fused. If we cut it this way, we are also forced to look at the structural issues like how open the system is at the point at which new people seek to join it. We must also look to how much they seek to change its values, and this must relate to how long they were closed out of the system.

Huntington:

I think that this is an interesting but different question. It is related to the extent that we can speak in experiential terms. On the other hand, the point is the presence or absence of experience.

Verba:

If I could follow that up for a moment, I think that there is a way in which entrants, of any sort, can fall under the same rubric. If we go back to the New Deal shift again, we will find evidence that it came from new entrants who were a combination of young people coming of age and immigrants who were first voting. They were similar if you use the notion that Burnham uses, a "political immunization." This is the notion that as people are more open to change their basic political attitudes or their basic political affiliation, the less experience they have had with the political system. The longer you've been in the system, the more rigid your views are. From that point of view, new entrants of any sort are those who are most easily moved by whatever are the experiences of the particular time. You can find this in all of the party affiliation data. In that sense both age and date of entrance into the system are equivalent to a certain extent.

Fine:

One kind of historian not included in this discussion is the revisionist historian. Whether or not you can explain the revisionist historians in terms of a generational model seems interesting to me. They essentially start from the assumption that they were going to go beyond liberalism, beyond the progressives to whom they were close, and certainly beyond the consensualists. The revisionists wrote a "new" type of history that really was not that at all. It was really back to Beard in a way. Their quarrel is with Schlesinger, Boorstein, and Hartz; they are coming out of the 1950s and 1960s. As an experiential generation, the revisionists do not experience the New Deal or World War II. Yet both the consensualists and the revisionists each write history in terms of their generation. Is there an explanation to be found here of the origins of paradigms or of models within the academic community itself? For example, in political science in the 1960s we have a back-to-Bentley movement. What I'm actually asking are two questions: Do the revisionists make a real effort to write a new history beyond liberalism? Or can they and the consensualists be subsumed under a generational source of modalities of thought and concept formation in such a way that in the end we get a conflict between institutions and ideals?

Huntington:

One point that your remarks suggest is the extent to which there is in academia some form of an interaction model at work where one generation is indeed reacting against another generation intellectually. This is what makes academic life interesting. I would suspect that the example of the revisionists versus the consensualists would not be wholly unsuited to this sort of analysis.

Dominguez:

I'd like to raise a simple operational point that can be tied into some of the other remarks that have been made here. One way to tie this in is by reference to your interchange with Sid Verba concerning the John Field hypothesis—that is, how can one distinguish among the three generational explanations that you've outlined? Sid Verba had suggested that in the case of the John Field experience that some of these explanations were cumulative. You responded by saying that it was an experiential one. That leads me to wonder how to operationally distinguish among these models. Two examples: In your remarks you had said that the 1920s generations tended to be conservative, that the New Deal generation tended to be more liberal, and that the generation of the 1940s and 1950s tended to be more conservative again. You posited that as an example of an experiential explanation. It seems to me, on the basis of what you've just said, that one could say that that is also amenable to an interaction explanation.

Huntington:

On that point, one would think of the interaction of children versus parents. In the example we are speaking of, however, generations are separated by only some ten years. We are speaking of when people entered politics. It would be hard to argue that the people who entered politics in the 1930s were reacting against their elder siblings who entered politics in the 1920s. You could say perhaps that they were reacting against their parents, who had entered politics in the Teddy Roosevelt years, but then that kind of interaction would not account for the decade-by-decade shifts. The experiential model would be better for that.

Dominguez:

If we look at your data in Table 2-2 for the people born in 1924-1931 and look across horizontally, we would see a maturation explanation, where their scores fall from 79 percent to 44 percent. If we look diagonally—that is, if we look at the experiential explanation of those who are 21-28 years old— that falls from 79 percent to 37 percent. The drop diagonally, the experiential explanation, seems to be more pronounced than the drop horizontally, which would be a life cycle explanation. If you compare the horizontal and diagonal lines, in each case there is consistently a more pronounced experiential drop than the life cycle drop. Is this the kind of argument that you're making?

Huntington:

That is exactly the point I was making. It seems to me that this data suggest the explanatory power of the experiential model, but not only in the way you've pointed out. Also, in the sense that people *do* get immunized at an early age. There is a fixation set at an early age. The likelihood of a change in attitudes as one gets older decreases. Nonetheless, some people change. You could interpret the change on the horizontal line as being a powerful experience that hit some of these people when they were in their thirties or forties.

Weiner:

The critical element of the experiential thesis is that there are differential effects of experiences on different generations. That would explain why a war obviously affects some generations more than others. Questions of health policies or busing have different effects on one generation than on another. That brings us to the issue with which we grappled earlier. You ended by trying to indicate that the generational conflict theories seem to be especially relevant to the United States. But it seems to me that the more you argue for an experiential model, the more that case somehow becomes weaker.

Huntington:

You could say that experiences had a more dramatic effect on different genera-tions, and on younger generations in particular, if factors of class, status, and so forth are less important. In other words, this is so if these people are less committed, less involved in looking at politics from their particular occupation or from their location in the social structure, as distinguished from a particular location in time.

Schneider:

I think that it is good to end here because I'd like to mention the work that I think does the best job on generational analysis, Butler and Stokes (1971). I think that it answers a lot of questions. We've talked about why generations may not be noticeable, and why generational conflict doesn't explain class conflict. They do a generational analysis by cohorts of the British electorate, and they find that generations are very important in explaining British politics, just as they might explain politics in the United States.

Two things are very important here in terms of explanatory power. The experience of mass politics is much longer in the United States than it is in any other country. In most other countries it is dated from the 1920s. This means that there haven't really been very many generations. Secondly, most conflicts in politics are not generational conflicts; they are conflicts by class, region, and ethnicity. Generation is not a conflict, which is why it doesn't appear in the newspaper every day. In the majority of cases, generations don't *make* conflicts, they *transmit* them. That is what the U.S. data has shown, and that is what the Butler and Stokes data has shown. British politics is about class. Nevertheless they use a cohort analysis, a generational model, to show how political generations transmit the politics of class with greater or lesser intensity, depending on the experience of each generation. That is why I think generations explain a lot, as in Butler and Stokes' analysis, but you don't see them in the newspapers every day because that is not what politics is all about.

References

Allison, Graham. 1970-71. "Cool It: The Foreign Policy of Young America." *Foreign Policy*, no. 1 (Winter), pp. 144-60.

Butler, David, and Stokes, Donald. 1971. *Political Change in Britain*. New York: St. Martins Press.

Foner, Anne. 1974. "Age Stratification and Age Conflict in Political Life." *American Sociological Review*, vol. 39 (April).

Harris, P.M.G. 1969. "The Social Origins of American Leaders: The Demographic Foundations." *Perspectives in American History*, vol. III, pp. 159-346.

Klingberg, Frank L. 1952. "The Historical Alternation of Moods in American Foreign Policy. *World Politics*, vol. IV (January), pp. 239-73.

Marsh, Alan. 1975. "The 'Silent Revolution,' Value Priorities, and the Quality of Life in Britain." *American Political Science Review*, vol. 69 (March).

Schlesinger, Arthur M. 1964. *Paths to the Present*. Boston: Houghton Mifflin.

Stone, Lawrence. 1972. *The Causes of the English Revolution, 1529-1642*. New York: Harper and Row.

Verba, Sidney, and Nie, Norman H. 1972. *Participation in America: Political Democracy and Social Equality*. New York: Harper and Row.

3

Generational Change Among Black Americans

Martin Kilson

We should begin this discussion of generational change among black Americans by referring to Huntington's work on political generations in this volume. It points clearly, more than any other work that I've seen on the political sociology of generations, to the determining role of generational clusters. Indeed, the generational cluster is seen as almost equivalent to social class as a carrier of change. My feeling is that this view may be taking the generational hypothesis a bit too far. In elevating the political generation to the level of causal agent, I fear that it takes on a disembodied quality. It becomes difficult to identify the next level, unlike the way we are able to specify continuity with the model of social classes. What are the institutions that shape a generation? What gives a generation continuity across time and space? In order to be a determinant of politics as has been implied, it would have to possess such a continuity.

A lot of the influence that we might attribute to generations might be only symptomatic of something else. I have a hunch that what we identify as a generation is really a failure of more institutionally specific belief-influencing and belief-changing mechanisms. Whenever there seems to be a generational factor visible we are probably looking at the failure of some socializing agent that is precluding the formation of a smooth transfer from one generation to the next.

The generational problem is a very tricky one, for you can get some degree of uniformity in generational behavior along one axis even while it will have substantial continuity with what has always been the case on another axis. An example is that of the young people in the 1960s who chose to wear long hair. We saw evidence of changing sexual attitudes for example; yet they still preferred Nixon over Humphrey. There was still by and large continuity with the political mainstream. Even though attitudes on general ideological questions seemed to have changed, these were not translated into a fundamentally discontinuous political profile. This is the case even though we know that the generation of the 1960s was different from generations that preceded it. My point, therefore, is that while I think there is some utility in the generational model, it has its limitations.

We can see evidence of how highly variable the generational hypothesis is if we take a quick look at a recent issue of *Ebony Magazine* (1976) for example. It has photographs in it of every homecoming queen at about sixty Negro colleges. As I looked at the photos I was struck by the fact that a large number (70 percent) of these homecoming queens had their hair pressed, straightened as if in deference to a larger white culture. It occurred to me that if I had looked at the 1969 collection of *Ebony's* homecoming queens I would have found almost every woman wearing her hair in an Afro style. This was the time of the young black generation's attempts to forge a sharp discontinuity with the larger society.

There obviously was something of a generational factor among blacks in the United States. What the 1960s displayed was this effort at discontinuity with the broader culture, both black and white. The effort was led by young blacks. My data show this fact quite clearly, but the analytic question is: What does it mean? Is the young generation capable of institutionalizing these new conceptions of how blacks should proceed? Does the generational difference also imply an extensive and sharply etched institutional difference with regard to socialization processes in general and with regard to political institutional processes in particular?

The answers appear quite ambiguous as we take a look at the data in Table 3-1. We can see a different profile between attachments toward separatism and attachments toward integration. This is a fundamental question. The same people who will score highly on some general separatist profile will retreat toward the middle on this more institutionalizing kind of preference.

If we begin to ask why the discrepancy, we may find some interesting answers on the Table 3-2, which deals with black perceptions of specific white institutions, as against white America in general; the profile of generation as discontinuity begins to dissolve.

Table 3-1
Black Attitudes Toward Separatism and Integration (percent)

Responses to the question, "Do you agree or disagree that Negroes can get what they want only by banding together as black people against the whites, because the whites will never help Negroes?"

Total Sample	1963	1966	1969				
Agree	x	25	27				
Disagree	x	64	59				
Not sure	x	11	14				

North	Total	Under 30	30-49	50 and Older	Low Income	Low Middle	Middle Income
Agree	30	45	26	25	22	34	32
Disagree	54	43	57	61	47	56	53
Not sure	16	13	17	14	32	10	15

Source: Peter Goldman (and Gallup Poll), *Report from Black America* (New York: Simon and Schuster, 1970). Reprinted with permission.

Table 3-2
Black Attitudes Toward White Institutions (percent)

Responses to the items, "Now I want to give you a list of different people and groups that are run by white people. Do you think _____ have been more helpful or more harmful to Negro rights?"

	Age		
	Under 35 1966	35-49 1966	50 and over 1966
White Churches			
More helpful	27	31	33
More harmful	18	16	15
Not sure	55	53	52
Local Police			
More helpful	22	26	30
More harmful	41	33	28
Not sure	37	41	42
Labor Unions			
More helpful	41	45	46
More harmful	15	13	11
Not sure	44	42	43
White Businesses			
More helpful	25	31	40
More harmful	27	18	13
Not sure	48	51	47

Source: Peter Goldman (and Gallup Poll), *Report from Black America* (New York: Simon and Schuster, 1970), pp. 253-4. Reprinted with permission.

My point here is this: There is something that is very conducive to change in generational clusters as such, but I would argue that it is conducive only in a relatively risk-free, cost-free context. When we ask questions concerning the willingness of black individuals to accept membership in unions run by George Meany, for example, at that point the generational model does not seem to be particularly significant. It does not then appear to be a discontinuity-pyramiding mechanism. It becomes either ambiguous, or it just breaks down. There seems to be no significant generational differentiation when you confront young blacks with concrete institutional alternatives.

It is my hunch that the significance of generational differences among blacks has already crested. It seems to be becoming highly diffused and thus is losing whatever mobilizing capacity it had developed in a counterestablishment context. There is no evidence that it will be otherwise, given of course the absence of a cataclysmic event.

Discussion

Pye:

There is an issue that should be raised concerning elite generations. Your data is useful in helping us to get a handle on mass attitudes differentiated by generations. But what of generational divisions with the black leadership? Can we identify, for example, a passing of the baton from the clergy to a more secular leadership? If so, how do leaders build their power in the absence of a congregation of followers?

Kilson:

There is a problem here in that blacks have not been a group with parity in the professions, for example. The black legal profession is really just beginning to take hold. There are now about 4,200 black law students. Before 1960, there were produced annually only about 200 black lawyers, and only about 100 black physicians. At the level of the political system, blacks have not long been involved in our major agencies and institutions, at least not to the extent that we can identify generational processes at work. Until 1950, some 70 percent of American blacks were still in the South. The shift to a small majority of blacks living outside the South (51.5 percent) occurred within the 1950–1970 period. I should add parenthetically that now there has emerged a net return to blacks to the South.

Now, blacks *have* been in the political process in a minuscule way outside the South, of course. In 1940, only 5 percent of black adults were permitted to register as voters in the South. In the non-South blacks have had a longer experience of access to the political process. Yet this access has mushroomed in the last fifteen years. In 1960 there were some 100 to 150 black elected officials in the entire United States. Today there are approximately 4,500; about 1.5 percent of all elected officials are now black. But I would argue that if you compared the political leadership styles, methods, and appeals of this new group with those of the group that Gosnell (1935) studied in Chicago, you would not find much discontinuity. You will find appeals to racial militancy by Edward Wright, Oscar DePriest, and Archibald Carey and other subjects of this study that do not differ substantially from what obtains today.

As far as a shift from clerical to secular leadership is concerned, I am again not sure that we can identify a generational division. Mays and Nicholson (1933) did a study, called *The Negro's Church*, that demonstrated something which was quite well-known about the Negro clergy: The Negro clergy has always been secular. Only at the fringe of the Negro clergy, only at the store-front level, do we have something that is more exclusively other-worldly. The established clergy, whether Methodist or Baptist, always had a very high secular profile. The Mays and Nicholson book showed that long before whites came to use their churches for dances and other secular gatherings, the black churches were doing this.

The new black leadership will build its power within an institutional context. At the moment, the 25 percent of the blacks who can properly be identified as part of the stable working class have an incidence of trade unionization that is 10 percentage points higher than that of whites; 37 percent of the black working class is trade unionized. This is how blacks will get politicized, and it is no different than it is for whites.

Pye:

Doesn't that imply then that the black leadership will be very much like the white leadership?

Kilson:

Yes indeed; that's true, and this is part of the problem of the generational model. The generational axis for a black appears simultaneously with the opening of the normal agencies of power and influence in the larger society. If you look at the rise of trade unionism, for example, as Purcell (1960) did in the meat-packing industry, you will find blacks penetrating unions during and after World War II. In this period blacks are beginning to penetrate the institutions that are coterminous with their occupational positions. By the 1960s, we had this curious dichotomy: On the one hand, blacks were included, at a low-profile level, in the powerful institutions of society; on the other hand, at the attitudinal level, there was a fierce, highly emotive movement seeking to wrench something *black* from the larger society. But this was short-lived.

The important shift, to the extent that it is important, is a mass shift, not an elite one. There is nothing fundamentally new in black leadership, save undoubtedly that blackness has a greater symbolic visibility.

Rangarajan:

On the leadership question a point emerges from Kluger's (1976) book *Simple Justice* that the perception of the black leadership toward securing rights from the white majority has changed in generational terms. The book is contemptuous of the Tuskeegee philosophy. This was the early view that sought to avoid change for fear of distorting and jeopardizing the black situation. This seemed to change to the NAACP philosophy, which in turn gave way to the Thurgood Marshall philosophy that the judicial system held the promise of justice for black America. What followed was the more militant Eldridge Cleaver style of confrontation as a mechanism to force change. Now I presume that William Coleman is the symbol of having arrived. Is there not a generational change here?

Kilson:

In each generation there will surely be something new, but if one is to really validate the generational model one would have to argue that the generation is the source of a distinct and ongoing discontinuity. *More than that, it must also be a discontinuity that in time becomes relatively generalized and pervasive within a group. It must surmount and displace all other divisions.* In the case of the black leadership this has not happened. For example, Booker T. Washington had not been discredited at all; indeed a lot of his ideas, such as self-help, were adopted in the 1960s. He has an entirely new status among blacks, even within the separatist group. In each new generation we will find new input, as DuBois had something that Washington did not quite have; yet DuBois did not displace Washington.

I can give you an example from a recent unpublished Ford Foundation study of medical students that asked questions concerning their plans for the first few years of medical practice. The white students outdistanced the black students by three to one with regard to their intention to spend time in providing medical assistance to the poor. This survey was done three or four years ago, and thus these black students were coming to adulthood in the period of generational differentiation among blacks. Yet they differ little from older generations of black doctors who aggressively maximized their wealth-earning capacity and paid little attention to needs of the black poor.

Weiner:

What you are calling attention to is the bifurcation in the black community between the growing educated middle and upper sectors on the one hand and the large community of the black unemployed on the other. Is there a problem here of an even sharper cleavage within the black community among people of the same generation who are poles apart in the class structure and in their capacity to take advantage of the new opportunities?

Kilson:

This is certainly the case. Recently, for the first time, small but growing numbers of this new black elite are openly confronting the issue of crime in the black community. There are also new voices being raised concerning the breakdown of authority and discipline in the schools where lower-class black students predominate. There is clearly a class cleavage that cuts across generation, and it is growing. It results from the fact that during the past fifteen years blacks have experienced enormous rates of upward mobility and moved into levels of educational, occupational, and wealth attainment hitherto unprecedented. This mobility, moreover, cuts deep into the black lower strata and has successfully reduced the proportion of black poor from 60 percent of the black population in 1950 to 32 percent today. Thus despite the intensification of black feelings about white racist constraints upon entry into American society and upon greater black definition of their place in the society, a vast majority of blacks have opted for the American mainstream and for these patterns of life that predominate in the American mainstream. We are now in a period when more and more blacks feel they can articulate this preference for the mainstream, which is precisely what the new thrusts among working-class and middle-class blacks against black crime represent. There is no reason to expect a reversal in this very important development.

Huntington:

I'd like to go back to the data for a moment. The thought was noted that the significance of generational differences among blacks had already crested. Yet there is a residue left of these generational splits, which are revealed in Table 3-3. As shown in the table, differences between blacks under thirty and over fifty in terms of willingness to go to jail (45 percent to 19 percent) and willingness to picket a store (59 percent to 25 percent) seem to be substantial. It seems to me that the interesting question is: What will be the attitudes of those who were under thirty when this poll was taken when they are over

Table 3-3
Black Attitudes on Militancy (Percent)

North	Total	Under 30	30-49	50 and Older	Low Income	Low Middle	Middle Income
Take part in a sit-in	43	57	47	27	25	45	53
March in a demonstration	49	63	51	36	28	51	62
Picket a store	43	59	47	25	29	46	55
Stop buying at a store	56	67	56	44	44	57	66
Go to jail	32	45	35	19	16	31	43

Source: Peter Goldman (and Gallup Poll), *Report from Black America* (New York: Simon and Schuster, 1970) p. 242. Reprinted with permission.

fifty? We have discussed the relative importance of the life cycle interpretation versus an experiential interpretation of generational formation. Will these younger, more militant blacks maintain their militancy as the experiential hypothesis would suggest? Or will they become more moderate, as the life cycle hypothesis would lead us to expect?

Kilson:

We ought not overlook the fact that institutions and roles can become determinant at some point. Firebrand anticapitalists who may decide upon a career in law or engineering will undoubtedly mellow in their attitudes. New situations such as parenthood or residential choice can play enormous roles in shaping attitudes.

My hunch is that there certainly will be change, but that the range and scale of discontinuity over time is not going to be comparable to what our surveys reveal. Thus, the maturation, or life cycle, model seems reasonable.

Pye:

What do you think is going to be the reaction of a generation that is aware of affirmative action? Is there going to be a generational division between this group and their fathers who felt that they had to fight a battle to overcome their disadvantages? Is there going to be a problem within the generation that may not be able to discern whether or not they faced a situation that was stacked in their favor?

Kilson:

The answer to your question has to stem from the recognition of the fact that although black Americans have had a unique historical experience, they are also very much Americans—that is, most Americans share a "get-in-as-get-in-can" orientation. After all, if we look at the data on the rise of the Irish-American middle sectors, we will find a larger number of them with public policy or government connected employment than any other ethnic group. Terry Clark (1975), at Chicago, is doing work on this, and he shows that where a lot of Irish Catholics (or any other immigrant group) are dominant, we will find an expanded bureaucracy. Jobs will be created. It was not called affirmative action, it was called spoils. So I don't expect any greater self-doubt among this generation of blacks than among any other ethnic generation that has benefited from ascriptive advancement.

References.

Clark, Terry N. 1975. "The Irish Ethic and the Spirit of Patronage." *Ethnicity*, vol. 2 (June).

Ebony, April 1976.

Gosnell, Harold. 1935. *The Negro Politician*. Chicago: University of Chicago Press.

Kluger, Richard. 1976. *Simple Justice*. New York: Knopf.

Mays, Benjamin E., and Nicholson, Joseph W. 1933. *The Negro's Church*. New York: Institute of Social and Religious Research.

Purcell, Theodore. 1960. *Blue Collar Man: Patterns of Dual Allegiance in Industry*. Cambridge, Mass.: Harvard University Press.

4

Fathers and Sons and Daughters and National Development

Harold R. Isaacs

While the inclusion of daughters in the title of this chapter would seem to be required by our new postsexist grammar, it can hardly be avoided now that Indira Gandhi has provided us with such a peculiarly dramatic illustration of our theme, which has to do with the passage of power and place from the nationalist to the postnationalist, the preindependence to the postindependence generation in the postcolonial countries of Asia and Africa.

Acting under the same powers the British had used to imprison Mahatma Gandhi and her father, Jawaharlal Nehru, and thousands of their Congress followers in the years of the nationalist struggle, Indira Gandhi sent her police out in the early morning hours of a June day to arrest some of her father's best-known surviving prisonmates of that time—J.P. Narayan, Moraji Desai, Ashoka Mehta—and thousands of others who were her political critics and opponents. She muzzled the press, barred free assembly, and subsequently had her docile majority in parliament set aside all constitutional and legal hindrances to the indefinite continuation of her newly established one-woman rule. She acted, even as the British had, against the threat of "chaos" brought on by "agitation" and "conspiracy." The agitation and conspiracy was an open call by a loose and not very effective opposition coalition to launch a civil disobedience campaign on the Gandhian model aimed at ending Indira Gandhi's tenure as prime minister, which was something that had already been ordered by an Indian court—also a legacy from the British—after she had been found guilty of election irregularities. After her coup, Mrs. Gandhi had her parliament vote the retroactive repeal of the statutes under which this finding had been made and place her and other top officials of the government beyond the reach of any law or court action. The authoritarian impulses Nehru had once located as seeded in his Kashmiri Brahmin self came this way to flower—if that is quite the word—in his daughter. And by her side as her most intimate advisers, some reports say, have been her two sons—especially the younger son Sanjiya—whose own father Indira had long before put aside so that she could stand next to and eventually succeed her father. Mrs. Gandhi adds the stuff of intense psychodrama to what is so much more broadly such a visible part of the common political generational experience in the excolonies.

That such a prime current example should lie in India just now is also peculiarly apt for the purposes of this chapter (which was also originally intended as a contribution to a *festschrift* in honor of A.D. Gorwala). At age 75, A.D. Gorwala is one of the more visible and articulate survivors of that prenationalist corps of elite Indian civil servants created by the British to help them govern India. There are those, contemplating the morass in which the country now flounders, who would argue that the old I.C.S. gave India the best administration it had ever had, before the British time or since. After first trying and failing to serve the new independent Indian government in the same way (he found he could not play the politics required or blink away the corruption it generated), Gorwala became a kind of one-man opposition—that is, a loyal but unrelentingly sharp critic of the Congress regime in all its incarnations since the passing of the British Raj. I do not know whether Gorwala is among those jailed by Indira Gandhi, but it is not hard to guess at what some of his mixed feelings might be about the matter. Age and ill-health and prison conditions apart, Gorwala would fully savor the ironies of the outcome: the prenationalist unjailed in the British time, free after independence to voice and publish his views of the corruption, witlessness, and inefficiency in government, finally caught in the toils of the postnationalist heirs to power, jailed or otherwise silenced along with aging Gandhians, younger would-be Gandhians, democrats, socialists, Hindu conservatives, anti-Muscovite Communists, and other assorted radicals, British-style civil libertarians, judges, lawyers, editors, writers, all shackled or gagged together far more effectively by the new Indian raj (or rani?) than they ever were in the British time.[a]

Under the British Raj, a massive nationalist movement grew despite repression and finally prevailed. Under Indira or her successors, rather different styles of repression and of responding politics are much more likely to shape further outcomes. I happened to visit India early this year, not long after Mujib in Bangladesh had closed down what remained there of open politics and installed government by one-man decree. It was common in conversations about politics in New Delhi at that time for someone to wonder out loud whether Indira would try to find her way out of her sea of troubles by going the "Mujib way." Which indeed in June she did. But in Bangladesh in August the "Mujib way" led Mujib to the end of it all, murdered in his home by a band of young officers. In Bangladesh, as in so many other places in postcolonial Asia and Africa, politics became not a matter of contending parties or any form of popular consultation and expression, but of the frequent and more or less bloody replacement of politicians and soldiers in the seats of power each in his turn sending his police and soldiers out in the middle of the night, as Indira began doing in June, to dispose of critics and opponents and rivals, with a bemused or indifferent

[a]Gorwala managed to keep his one-man journal of dissent, *Opinion,* publishing until August 1976, when he was finally forced to cease publication. In his letter to his 2,000 subscribers announcing the end of *Opinion,* Gorwala wrote: "The current Indira regime, founded on June 25, 1975, was born through lies, nurtured by lies, and flourishes on lies. The essential ingredient of its being is the lie. Consequently, to have a truth-loving, straight-thinking, plain-speaking journal examine it week after week and point out its falsehood becomes intolerable to it."

population barely looking on or even noticing the change in cast of characters at the top. The question now is perhaps not whether but how far India will go down that road. Whether Mujib's fate has given Indira pause or she otherwise finds some other more profitable and even "democratic" way of pursuing her present course remains to be seen.

In the few months since these events in Bangladesh and India, successful coups have taken place in Nigeria and Peru and abortive coups in Ecuador and the Sudan. Nigeria's chief of state, General Gowon, was displaced from power in Lagos even as he sat in his influential seat at a conference of African states in Kampala hosted by Idi Amin, who came to power in Uganda by coup and has put down countless countercoups since. In Peru, a general in power was replaced by another general while the Peruvian government was hosting a conference of nearly one-hundred members of the "nonaligned" bloc, almost as if to remind them that the prime model for their politics was made in Latin America, where coup-countercoup and a succession of petty dictators has been the postnationalist way of life for about a hundred and fifty years, ever since that continent went through its nationalist struggles, heard the lofty call to freedom, and won its independence from Spain.

Nationalist movements have of course varied greatly in their courses and their outcomes. The Chinese and Vietnamese experiences stretched out over nearly a century or more of wars and revolutions before ending in the establishment of national-communist regimes on the Russian model. Half a century or so of quite different kinds of political struggle produced a government and a political system in India modeled essentially on the British and in the Philippines on the American. European metropolitan frameworks shaped the new national regimes that came into existence in much of Africa—in most of them after only a few years of nationalist ferment or, indeed, as in Belgian and almost all of French Africa, after none at all. Most of this scaffolding has been demolished since; with all their differences all these regimes now share, in greater or lesser degree, government by closed politics of one kind or another that ranges all the way from an effective total system of control and social mobilization, as in China, to ineffectual little satrapies maintained only by a bloody-handed palace guard, as in Uganda.

But if this is what they share in the end, there was something else that those rooted in nationalist movements all shared at the beginning. The nationalist fathers (and mothers) in the closing decades of the European colonial era could embrace a "pure" cause, full of valid emotion, undeniable virtue, and unassailable values: self-respect, self-determination, rejection of imposed racial/cultural inferiority, a reach for equality of status with the loved/hated foreign ruler. The fight against the white supremacy system in the American society had the same character. These were almost the last "pure" causes of our era. European imperialism could be defended only on grounds of naked rapacity and an assumption of racial/cultural superiority supported and maintained by physical and psychological force. These were indeed the underpinnings of Western empire in Asia and Africa as of white supremacy in America, whatever the accompanying rationalizations having to do with economic development, "modernization," or soul-saving or "civilizing" goals. But these sources of Western power were heavily seeded, as Mao might say, with self-destroying contradictions. The rhetoric of colonial counterassertion of human worth and equal political rights came not out of any of the autocratic and tyranny-ridden political traditions of victimized Asia and Africa but out of the revolutionary, liberal, humanistic, and nationalistic countertraditions of Europe itself.

The youthful Sun Yat-sen's hero and model was Abraham Lincoln. The youthful Nehru thrilled at Harrow to Trevelyan's account of Garibaldi and he dreamed of "similar deeds in India." When he ultimately put on the mantle of power, Nehru had much more in common with the man he took it from, Lord Mountbatten, than he did with Gandhi with whom he shared the nationalist leadership in an uneasy and often baffling relationship. In the nationalists who eventually challenged them in colony after colony, the still rapacious and arrogant Europeans and Americans met their own superego selves, repeating the profession of their own proudly hailed histories, quoting their own best-remembered words back at them. In their proclamation of independence in September 1945, the Vietnamese charged the French with abusing the ideal of liberty, equality, and fraternity, and quoted from both the American Declaration of Independence and the French Declaration of the Rights of Man of 1971. In Indonesia, the nationalists—who expected American troops to be arriving when Japan surrendered—scrawled on their walls the proposition that "all men are created equal" and announced that they were seeking no more than "life, liberty, and the pursuit of happiness."

With their wars and other assorted "contradictions," the imperialists in the end did most to bring about their own downfall. High and sharp among the petards on which they hoisted themselves were their own professions about freedom and the dignity, not to say the brotherhood, of man. The use of these ideas and phrases by some nationalists, especially in 1945, was in part shrewdly calculated fun-and-games on their part. But it remains a fact nevertheless that their own dreams of power and pelf had to be draped in these flowing periods. Along with all kinds of other spurs to action, these were the ideas that mobilized their movements and inspired the parties and individuals who finally made it possible for these leaders to sit in the seats of the mighty vacated by their predefeated foreign rulers. It is no forgettable fact that every new nationalist regime that came into being in these decades—even the communist, which marched to a different but nevertheless also a European drummer's beat—has had these ideas inscribed on its banners and incorporated in its constitution.

The nationalist fathers (and mothers) had, then, their pure, beautiful, driving cause that was rooted in the universal imperatives of group pride, cultural chauvinism, and the desire for material gain transformed, via the European exposure, into ideas of political nationhood and democratic freedoms. These are what inspired the young and made it possible for them to see themselves in the best and brightest of all possible lights. They gave a euphoric quality to youthful hopes and provided a liturgy for their devotions—a reason for sacrifice. They made the nationalist period a time to risk all, whether over long years or even in a brief moment that could become the finest, and most nostalgically remembered moment of a lifetime.[b]

Whatever the many varieties of individual experience, it was the political and emotional breadth of the nationalist appeal that became its most powerful feature. One way or another, its drives and motivations could touch everyone in the colonial societies. It could cut across the deep social, economic, and political, and in some cases generational cleavages. It made even the largely nonparticipating mass of people the sea in which the nationalist fish could safely swim. Stories of the beginnings of nationalist movements and the lives of nationalist leaders usually begin with rebellious sons rejecting the submissive ways of their fathers. In China this became a break not only and not even primarily in the beginning from submitting to foreign domination but from the whole encrusted social and political order of the past, far more so, incidentally, than it ever was in India, thereby perhaps accounting in part for the different outcomes in these two key countries. But in both countries, as elsewhere, the cause of nationalism as a political movement offered itself as a cause that rose above differences of class, caste, cultural group, or political ideology. Pre-World War I nationalist movements were generated in the upper and middle classes: Some fathers had begun to acquire an economic stake in more effective competition with the dominant foreigners and the sons had begun to act at home on the libertarian, egalitarian, nationalist ideas they had encountered during their European and American schooling. Members of both generations felt that first strong breeze of possible change in 1905 when Japan's victory over Russia suddenly showed them that dreams could come true. The schoolboy Nehru felt it, as did hosts of others of his generation. The event drew thousands of young Chinese and other Asians to Japan; They were sent by their fathers to learn how they might travel the same path.

The even stronger wind that blew out of Russia in 1917 quickened these early trickling streams of nationalism in Asia. It brought with it the new and more aggressive style of revolutionary politics that in certain countries after

---

[b] I think of an Indian banker I met in the late 1950s who had such a moment in his life, in 1942, when he was drawn by the turmoil in the August demonstrations that year, was arrested and spent some days in jail, to the horror of his banker father who promptly sprung him and put him on the right path, from which he did not stray again. But that was clearly the experience that counted for him in his estimate of himself and gave him, he said, a concept that there was an *India* to which he had to devote himself. Now he had two growing sons and neither one of them, he said sadly, cared about *India*. "They only care about themselves."

1920—China, Vietnam, Indonesia—began to split radical nationalist sons in much harsher ways from conservative nationalist or traditionalist fathers. Communist parties appeared to the left of the existing older nationalist political parties armed with the new Comintern idea that the "bourgeois-democratic" revolution had become the task of communist-nationalists in those countries where the proletariat was still too weak to make a revolution of its own. Nationalist politics in the 1920s became—whether with deep Russian involvement, as in China, or without it, as in India—an alliance of contending parties and interests across class and ideological lines. In their different ways, the Kuomintang-Communist Party alliance in China and the Congress movement in India provided the broad nationalist umbrella under which everyone could gather, blurring or deferring the pressing issues of the further development of the society until the great primary national cause could be won.

It is worth remarking here that it was their relation to the national cause that determined how the various parties involved in these struggles came out in the end. The Communist Party never did become a significant force in Indian nationalist politics. The Congress Party embraced the whole political spectrum, all the more as Gandhi threw over it his aura, the *darshan* of his own special religious/evangelical character of avoiding all serious commitment to fundamental political/social/economic change; Gandhi was slow in coming even to the idea of independence from Britain and his emphasis on changing the human soul could be welcomed by many who did not want to change much else that might be more readily changeable. The left wing of the Congress, represented by the Congress socialists and Nehru's League-Against-Imperialism brand of fellow-travelerism never did seriously threaten the primacy of the politically and socially conservative right wing leadership that could always rely on Gandhi to stand with them whenever hard social issues did intrude upon the nationalist struggle. But it was the Communist Party's abandonment of the nationalist cause to support the war on Russia's behalf after June 1941 that doomed it to remain a negligible, or at least subordinate or secondary, factor in Indian nationalist politics, even until now.

In China, by contrast, and in Vietnam, it was ultimately the effective communist leadership of the nationalist cause that put the communists in power—in China when the war against Japan was won, and in North Vietnam, and, after twenty-five more years, when the French and then the Americans were finally forced to yield, in South Vietnam and the rest of Indochina. South Vietnam's political leadership in the interim came from groups and individuals that had never been identified with the nationalist cause in any serious way at all. Bao Dai had been a puppet emperor for the French, and Thieu, who finally rose to the top of the scrambling heap of contending politicians and generals, had been in the service of the French before becoming, as Chiang Kai-shek had in China and the hapless Diem in Saigon before him, a client of the Americans.

The political designs were differently woven in different places—Indonesia,

Burma, Ceylon, Algeria—and very differently indeed in most of later-coming Africa where with a few notable exceptions—Kenya, for one—national power was acquired without benefit of very much nationalism beforehand. But the point here is the simple but central one: For longer or shorter but always crucial periods, the national cause or the national idea overspread the internal divisions, conflicts, and difficulties, nascent or actual, in all the colonial societies. Whatever the sharpness of such divisions or intractability of the problems, the goal of achieving statehood overlay them all and could command the passions and summon up the heroic capabilities of all who embraced it. Wrapped in its flags, heroes and scoundrels could not easily be told apart. It drew on valid and powerful emotions as well as interests, and this is why it produced so many heroic or charismatic figures to carry it to its first limited conclusions.

An examination of the differences between the nationalist and postnationalist generations in the excolonies could very well begin with the fact that the nationalist experience produced leaders who could become and remain larger than life; some are, to be sure, larger than others—Sun Yat-sen, Ataturk, Gandhi, Nehru, Mao, Ho Chi-minh, and perhaps also, if he is not unfortunate enough to outlive his legend, Jomo Kenyatta. Smaller charismatic figures like Sukarno and Nkrumah whose evils as powerwielders so clearly outstripped whatever good they did as powerseekers, might nevertheless still manage not to have *all* their self-erected statues pulled down as time passes. Not larger than life but still candidates for canonization as fathers of their countries are men like Borguiba, who may have lived too long to save his reputation for sagacity, and Jinnah, who died almost too dramatically soon after creating possibly the most synthetic of the new nationalism of this century. They and others like them—Nasser, perhaps—might make some of the less famous or familiar additions to some lower rung of this gallery. Some founding fathers—Sekou Toure, Nyerere, Kaunda—are still at it; they are makers and leaders of nationalisms, sparce and feeble at best, struggling to cope with all their postnationalist problems. A few figures of this time passed by too fleetingly to be remembered as anything but fitful legends, and their survival depends possibly on what bards write what kind of songs about them in times to come: Aung San, Lumumba, Ben Bella are among the names that might appear when the time comes for the grandchildren of the postnationalist generation to discover who their heroes were. Frantz Fannon, who was not a leader at all but a tribune, may be remembered better than any of them. Even in this era of synthetic myth making and myth disposal and the highly developed technique of turning persons into nonpersons and events into nonevents, mythmakers in search of modern as well as ancient glories are going to have to settle for the best they can get. The cast of characters in tomorrow's nationalist histories will depend in no small part on who has disappeared down how many—and whose—memory chutes.

By contrast, the postnationalist or postindependence occupants of the seats of power are already for the most part a faceless lot. In China a small number of the old generation's leadership still rules, though not without crises, unexplained disappearances and reappearances: The whole world strains to discover who has gone to that shadowy Maoist limbo from which some now and then unaccountably return and who among the younger newcomers will occupy the places of power that must before too long finally fall vacant. In India, Mrs. Gandhi acquired visibility by inheritance and is now trying to retain it by keeping all possible rivals out of view. Most generally, however, as we scan the post-colonial scene at the top, few of the names stick and few of the faces become familiar, except where an individual here or there has won notice through some particular eccentricity, like the murderously erratic Amin or the predictably fanatic Quaddafi. It would be no more usual to be able to identify many of the others than to be able to name very many of the heirs of Bolivar, San Martin, or Juarez. It used to be a feat for American schoolboys (or girls) to be able to name all the presidents in order, and there have only been thirty-eight of them so far in 200 years. It would be much more of a feat, even for specialists in current African politics, to name all or even most of the current rulers in that continent's thirty-nine or forty countries, much less all who have ruled, coup after countercoup, during the less-than-twenty years of the era of independence.

In Asia takeovers of this kind still occur somewhat less frequently, at least as compared to Africa or Latin America, but postnationalist politics in Asia too have become essentially a matter of contenders or incumbents forcibly making or keeping room for themselves at the top: thus Burma, Pakistan, Indonesia, Thailand, South Korea, the Philippines; thus too now India and even more recently the newest of the "new" states, Bangladesh; thus too the states of the old Indochina, South Vietnam, Cambodia, and Laos, until they were taken over this spring, after decades of civil and interventionist wars, by the communists. In communist-ruled Asia greater stability at the top appears to be the more common rule, but the gap between appearance and reality is subject to the considerable communist ability to keep any instability up there from public view; it is one of the advantages of the remarkably closed politics of the communist system. At least one attempted coup and other crises of leadership have become partly visible in China but never clearly enough for the facts about them to be known or understood: the communist citadel in Peking is still a forbidden city for all but a chosen few. No comparably visible breaks have appeared in the seemingly stable facades of communist leaderships in North Korea and North Vietnam, but here again, we simply do not know how many opponents of any of these regimes and leaders rot in graves or in prison, much less know who they are.

Wherever we may place particular postcolonial regimes in the spectrum on the count of stability, the more important fact is the evolution of virtually all of these regimes into varieties of more or less authoritarian or closed political systems. The rhetoric of nationalist struggle invariably stressed the freedom that national independence would bring; in the happy-ever-after, the rule of the people would take the place of the tyrannies of colonialism. In the event, of course, the change came to mean freedom from foreign rule, not freedom from tyranny. The asserted role of the "people" in the so-called people's republics or people's democracies of the communist system was one of those exaggeratedly premature rumors taken at face value only by foreign friends and admirers of that system, by members of the lo-the-wonder-of-it-school of travelers to China and North Vietnam, and by radicals who, like the communists, literally or cynically confuse the "people" with themselves. The regimes fashioned on parts of this model in some of the excolonies, especially in Africa, were endorsed in their first years as "democratic" by some young American political scientists who apparently had needs and generational problems of their own. The euphemistic vagaries of Sukarno's "guided democracy" and Nkumah's "Nkrumahism" received sympathetic support in some of these quarters until it became too embarrassing even for them to continue it. There was often an initial effort made in some excolonies to hold on to the forms of open politics and government defined in the constitutions with which so many of them began their new statehood. But then, after intervals of shorter or longer duration, the pressures on the fragile structures became too great to bear: the push and pull of ambitious powerseekers and deeply divided groups—tribal, racial, linguistic, religious, regional—and the swift onset of unmanageable problems and demands with which the new regimes were neither politically nor administratively able or willing to cope. In one country after another the feeble attempt to realize government by free choice broke down and government by forced consent took its place. Varieties of one-party or no-party authoriarian political systems took place, the old colonial prisons filled up again, and closed politics became more and more the rule in the postcolonial world.

Until recently, the Philippines and India occupied the places at the most open end of the political spectrum: one with its American-style, deformed but nevertheless functioning, system of electoral politics and representative government going back to 1916; the other with its much briefer experience of democratic politics on the modified British model—amended by the creation of communal electorates—first tried out in India in the elections of 1937, producing the first but short-lived Congress government. That these forms lasted for twenty-six years in the independent Philippines and twenty-eight years in India nourished the illusion that some positive elements of the metropolitan influence had somehow stuck along with all the negative legacies of colonial power. But, as it turned out, the way of all colonial flesh lay before them too, the end lying only a little farther along. Three years ago in the Philippines Ferdinand Marcos showed that the American influence that was strongest there after all was the Latin American. And this year in India, the last walls of democratic politics in the postcolonial world collapsed: Mrs. Gandhi simply blew them down. It is the nature of closed political regimes that they keep us from knowing even as little as we knew before about what was going on; it may be too soon to judge how much actual or potential resistance to these coups there might be. But if the apparent absence of any effective resistance in both countries continues, it may be the final comment on just how super these democratic superstructures were, and how feeble and fragile the democratic political beginnings were even in these societies. Now, in any case, as in Communist Asia, India, and the Philippines too, the vox populi is no longer heard, not even the vague murmuring in which it came through until now; the vox dei is instead piped out to us on single government-controlled circuits, the one tuned baritone, the other soprano. As in Communist Asia, we now do not know how many political prisoners there are in the Philippines or India either. On the still partly open side of the postcolonial spectrum, only a few shaky bits and pieces of the scaffolding of open politics remain, as in Thailand, none of them with much promise of survival.

The passage from the generation of nationalist power seeking to national power wielding had to cross the great divide between nationalist dreams and national realities. There was really no other way to go. It was a passage for many, however, from a time when the romantic political imagination could thrive on the chance to experience dedication, devotion, commitment, heroism, and sacrifice. It took them into the waking nightmare of brutal self-seeking, frustration, paralyzing internal divisions and conflicts, and impotence that has filled most of their years since the nationalists drove the foreign rascals out and put their own native rascals in their place.

There was, after all, so little chance for it to be otherwise. Romantic nationalism got nowhere in Europe and it had nowhere to go in Asia and Africa once the walls of empire came tumbling down at its trumpet call. The new flags went up the flagpoles, some countries took new names, and some earnest efforts at change began, in education especially. But they brought so little so late to such enormous tasks. There was little or nothing in their past experience to support open politics, to assure the better exercise of "human rights," or to begin solving in any effective way the problems of their backwardness that came weighing down upon them. There was little or nothing of any of this in their past political or cultural experience, in the conditions and capabilities with which they emerged from colonial status, or in the jungle-like world situation into which they arrived to claim what they thought were their new places in the sun.

There may be much to mourn but little to wonder at, then, that so much fell and rotted along the way—like skulls or hulks in the desert—as they made the passage, wasting away all their hopes and promises of free popular government and greater respect for human worth. The fate of "human rights" along this way has been peculiarly painful—alas, poor rhetoric, we all knew it well. The reassertion of something called human dignity was at the heart of the nationalist demand for liberation from a status in which they and their people were so profoundly demeaned. It is easy to deal with this lightly or cynically if we did not know and share with a number of real, live, human beings the experience of taking these emotions seriously. But in the event, all each new national state had to do was sign the Universal Declaration of Human Rights, which they could thereafter invoke against others at their convenience at UN assemblies while themselves plunging on into the great bloodied shambles of political repression, internal group conflict, and mutual slaughter that has so largely filled so much of the postcolonial landscape in these years.

The promises of greater economic well-being that went with the nationalist program ran into blockages that in the final analysis were subject to wider international or world solutions far beyond the control of these feeble new national regimes. Unfortunately, they also remained beyond the reach of the great powers who had first to decide who would have the world in hand, a power struggle that imposed its pressures on all, forcing many to try to wriggle their way through to a condition called "nonaligned." They have before them the Chinese communist example of how to achieve a relative measure of improved mass well-being based on what might be called the ant-heap model made to work through a combination of positive reinforcements and total control. This was an example that most of the new states neither could nor would adapt for themselves, partly perhaps still because they shrink from *that* much control, but more because their patterns of capability and capacity, both economic and cultural, so vastly differed, and even more because the governing impulses of the new wielders of power in most of the excolonies run much more to the enrichment of the few, especially of themselves, and much less to easing the plight of the many.

Any reexamination of this recent and current history has to begin, it seems to me, with the recognition of its central paradox. Nationalism has remained the most powerful of all political drives even though it has long since become the most sterile of all political solutions in human affairs. Creating new states for themselves was the only political goal available to the subject peoples of the colonies even though the national state had long since ceased, in a globalizing world of power, resources, technology, and communications, to be in and by itself a viable instrument for effective social change. The limits and limitations of national power remain decisive still for large and small, powerful and weak, in a world that has so far been unable to generate any other kind of power to take its place.

An interim answer, then, is for the lesser states to try to run in packs: hence all the agglomerations of regional associations, of blocs and "nonaligneds." The new leverage recently brought to bear by the oil-producing states tries to rectify some of the imbalance by driving a harder bargain for the vital raw materials that the Westerners used to take almost at will but that the postnationalist states now control. This is obviously an attractive prospect for the latter, if only they can manage to control enough, and run in a pack long enough, to make any long-term difference. Those are big "ifs." As it is, the normal workings of human and political behavior intrude on the working out of new political-economic formulas. Its advantages are hugged close by what becomes a small new cluster of the favored-few who have pieces of the new bargaining power. They become what is now being defined as a somewhat shrunken "Third World," while a "Fourth World"—all the poorest countries who suffer even greater hardships and costs they cannot meet—is cut loose to float away like a great jammed ark that has nowhere to go, it seems, but down. Just what this newest postnationalist phenomenon holds in store waits to be seen. The course will be a long time running and new postnationalist generations will be taking it toward ends that are not now in view.

The effect of this experience on the generation of people who began this passage on the nationalist side of the gap, and on their sons and daughters, who are crossing it now to unknown destinations, will have to be studied in many different particular settings, among different people in different places. Some of the larger accompanying effects lie in what is taking place, meanwhile, in the educational systems of these countries—the windows through which further postnationalist generations are acquiring *their* picture of the world they did not make, of their own cultures, of their own places in the great confused mess of things. With all due respect to scholars, I suspect it will be the novelists who will finally tell us some of this story, if human society remains open enough to let them tell it.

But no one who has shared at least in this passage of years and who is still in touch with old friends of the nationalist time can fail to know some of the varieties of disenchantment, cynicism, and withdrawal that has been the fate of so many of them in the aftermath. Some are still driven as they were before, and end up finally, like the J.P. Narayans, in new blind alleys. Others, with exultant zest plunged themselves into the self-centered political or business careers that the winning of national power opened up to them; others—whether with pleasure or dismay—watched their sons and daughters do so, either with their help and approval, or against their helpless dissent and disapproval. True believers of the nationalist period who took its stated aims seriously fell on hard times in these years; here and there in government service or in other capabilities they tried to realize some of what they had wanted to bring about by other means, and many of them ended up in prison or in the varying limbos provided in different places for their kind.

Let me conclude with an illustrating anecdote about a Ghanaian I knew when he first came to this country about 1950 to try to discover what the new United Nations might have to offer by way of help to the unfolding nationalist hopes of people in his country. Some years later he returned as Ghana's ambassador to the United Nations and then later still was recalled by Nkrumah to Accra to take a high post in the government. But he found it impossible to follow Nkrumah on the way to becoming the Osagyefo, the Messiah, the Savior of the People. Because of long comradeship, he did not suffer the fate of others who became opponents of the Osagyefo but retired instead to his old school, where he had begun his career as a youthful Ghanaian nationalist, and this was where I found him one day in 1960—that was only three years after Ghana had gained its independence and was the summer when all the rest of West Africa was becoming "free." As we talked he got up at one point and beckoned me to the window. "See that shed down there," he said, pointing to a cluster of low buildings in the yard below. "That was where we used to keep our press. We would print out leaflets there, attacking the British, demanding our independence. Then we would go downtown to distribute them in the streets of Accra. Then," he said, eyes lit up with the bright memory of it, "*then* we were *free*!" Only a second or two later, with the sound of his words still hovering in the air between us, I thought he caught, from the expression on my face, the mirthless humor of what he had just said and shaking his head he turned from the window and went back to his desk. Today he is still trying to serve some useful cause in the role of an international civil servant. Now I think of how Gorwala would appreciate this story. Nationalist believers like my Ghanaian friend commonly met the same fate as the prenationalist Gorwalas. They either had to go along with how things were in the new real world or opt— or be opted—out.

Discussion

Pye:

It seems to me that the phenomenon of generations didn't really begin with the nationalists. It was also a phenomenon of the generation that produced the nationalists. It some respects, part of the fire of the nationalist generation was in that it was dealing with the preceding generation, either indigenous or foreign, that told them that their dreams were made of the air. The question is: Did the grandfathers predict things that their grandsons later confronted? Wasn't the fathers' generation merely an interlude between two generations that understood the harsh realities that you have referred to?

Isaacs:

I think that in order to confirm that particular generational pattern one would have to spell it out in a given context. In China, for example, there may have been differing degrees of acceptance and submission to the situation in the grandfathers' generation. In the China case we're speaking of a century, and there is certainly more than a fathers-and-sons generation. At no time, except for a tiny group of adapters, were there people who emotionally really accepted and internalized the foreign rulers. Generally speaking, even the comprador grandfathers hated the guts of the people they were accommodating to and whose power they were accepting. When their sons began to feel their oats and when their grandsons became revolutionists there was always an ambivalence—an ambiguous set of feelings that accompanied the emotions that were aroused by this. I don't recognize any situation in which either a grandfather or a conservative father spoke to this as legitimizing the status quo.

In the colonial situation there existed in different places anywhere from two to four or five generations. The reassertion of the attachment to one's own roots with whatever degree of pride or self-respect was the driving fuel of the nationalist movement. From the standpoint of traditional, chauvinistic group pride, as in the case of the Chinese, which then was given formulation by nineteenth-century European revolutionary rhetoric, this was what became the fuel of the nationalist movements of the last one hundred years. The greatest satisfaction one could have was in having one's own rascals oppressing one rather than having foreign rascals.

Bowie:

You've assessed the appeal to the liberal and Western aspects of the national movements, but there was also a considerable use of appeals to people lower down with grievances against the colonial situation. You don't really deal fully with this as one of the appeals used in the nationalist struggle. Secondly, I think that you ought to speak in greater detail about the inappropriateness of those institutions that were grafted to the newly independent states. Some of these parliamentary systems were merely picked up and placed down in areas to which they were wholly unsuited. There were no underpinnings for these institutions, so I wonder if these young states didn't start out with three strikes against them.

Isaacs:

That is of course quite correct. My response to your first point would be to note that there were grievances that moved beyond and below the level of the upper and middle classes in the colonial societies. In most of the places where there was a significant nationalist movement, there was a politics based upon competition with the foreigners. First came the desire to break out from under the control of the foreigner; the movement to more serious grievances was a phenomenon of later development. This was a phenomenon that came with the entry of the radicals and the communists into the picture. The turn to the grievances of the peasantry as a whole in China came after 1924—and did have the effect of mobilizing the politics in a wholly new way. In India, great efforts were made to avoid this, and most of the conflicts within the Indian national movement had to do with the push and pull of people who wanted to pursue effective social change and the Gandhian elements who sought to minimize that to appeal most directly to the question of foreign domination.

This varied enormously. In most of the places that you referred to there was no politics to speak of prior to the desperate attempt on the part of the retreating foreign rulers to get out of the way. It stands to reason then that the institutional setup was extremely fragile. Thus, all of these new politics were confronted from the outset with having to create for themselves, out of their own materials, whatever kinds of politics they could make of this situation.

Huntington:

There seem to be two important factors involved here. One is the transition from the nationalist generation to the postnationalist generation, that is, the passage of power from the charismatic leaders of the anticolonial movement to the "face-less lot" that followed. That is fair enough. But it also seems to me that there is running through this chapter the implication that the first generation was in some way more committed to ideals of liberalism and democracy than the following generation. One may reasonably wonder whether that is true. I don't think that it is. As I look over the list of nationalist leaders I don't see with but one excep-tion—that of Nehru—any individuals who were very committed to democracy or liberalism in any really meaningful sense. On the other hand, insofar as the following generation is concerned, it seems to me that the shift to the less demo-cratic forms of government in the Philippines and India, for example, may have less to do with the transition from one generation to another than it has to do with either phases in the process of development, or simply worldwide trends. After all, we've had the same phenomenon taking place in Latin American coun-tries, as in Uruguay and Chile, and this isn't a question of something else at work. There exists in this discussion an identification of the nationalist generation with democratic liberal ideals and the postnationalists with something different. Perhaps the second generation was not really as good as they've been made out to be here, and perhaps what has happened in the second generation may not have been because they were worse than their fathers.

Isaacs:

These charismatic leaders who represented the faces of the nationalist movements were not, and I don't think that I claimed that they were, thoroughly committed to popular sovereignty and democratic institutions. They were the people who expressed the valid emotions of the nationalist drive. They spoke with the pride of peoples who would no longer submit to foreign rule. They spoke to this whole pattern of self-assertion that I would argue was the main scheme and main thrust that got translated through the exposure to Western liberal notions into the language of political nationhood. That *did* remain mostly rhetoric. Most of these leaders did not promise liberal institutions, but only freedom from the yoke of foreign domination.

Weiner:

This chapter talks about generations in a biological sense, in the sense of fathers and sons and daughters. Other authors have suggested that we can conceive of political generations, as distinct from biological generations. The notion here is that cohorts are affected by common political experiences that take place in their society. There may be as a consequence of a series of major political events rather rapid changes in the number of political generations. If we look at it from that point of view, how would that affect the kinds of observations that have been made in this chapter?

Isaacs:

Here again, I suppose, one would have to go to any one of a number of specific cases. People who share especially critical events are indelibly marked by them. You have a very sharp demarcation of people in almost any critical era. They would constitute a generation very much like a class group, and I'm sure that there are times when this becomes very significant politically. In Burma, in the brief but intense national movement, such a generation appeared in the class of 1939 at the University. There was a group of young men all of whom took on the title of *thakin*, which means lord. It was an expression of their assertion of merit and of themselves. U Nu was known as Thakin Nu long before he became known as U Nu. This practice was gradually abandoned, but they became a very important class group identified in this way.

This concept of experientially-formed generations is of course not mutually exclusive with the idea of the biological generations, the fathers and sons and daughters, or by the kinds of experiences suggested by the data presented earlier. That is the fact that enormous percentages of the populations of all the new states are today between the ages of fifteen and thirty. These are people who have never had as part of their own experience the preindependence period. They have new mental landscapes. This raises the whole question of what I called one's "own" history, meaning the history that happens while a person is around and forms part of the life and times of which the person is a part. There is a real difference in the way in which we carry these things around.

Dominguez:

I can try to mistakenly argue that the issue of the nationalist generation in power is not really one of change between one generation and another, but that with some exceptions most of the changes that occur do so in a very short span of time among people of the same generation. They are struggling over other issues, whether they are ethnic struggles, or class struggles, or so forth. I could then try to pigeonhole these kinds of things that you have tried to cast in a generational framework in other kinds of approaches that I would be more familiar with. On the other hand, in the course of the discussion a number of possibilities have been thrown out by yourself and by others where there may be something to this generational argument. One of these was the idea that life cycle makes a predictable difference in terms of explaining political attitudes and political behavior. Perhaps the comparative study of the life cycles of individuals would be a way to get at some understanding of regularities that I could not get at if I had only these other frameworks.

Another possibility would be to look at how alternate generations have a number of things in common—that is, that grandfathers and grandsons have things in common that are opposed to those of the fathers' generation. There would be Mao and the Red Guards versus the bureaucrats in between, or any such other phenomenon in which one might say that there are psychological mechanisms that have certain regularities across society.

The third kind of argument is that there are certain experiences that groups share at a certain point in time that gives people an additional tie—an additional element of cohesion besides family or ethnicity or class. It seems to me that one of the tasks of scholarly endeavors is to say that there are these varieties of explanations, and that this one is slightly more important than that one. How do you yourself say just what is the efficacy of generational explanations as compared to the efficacy of explanations based on other kinds of work that you have done? Or, you can say that you can identify certain kinds of problems for which generational explanations don't make any sense at all?

Isaacs:

What you call the scholarly pursuit, in which you can have some commanding generalization that enables one to say that A is really more important than B, C, D, or E, is never like that in real life. I would go even a step further and say that the need to have some such overarching conviction is part of that tremendous need for security in knowing how one understands something. I suppose that that is part of the scholarly endeavor, but it is also a part of all religion, part of all ethnic identity, and part of all the different ways in which we create systems by which we understand the mysteries of life. Everything is so mixed and so ambiguous, that the real intellectual problem is how to deal with the ambiguities, how to deal with the cases that don't fit, how to accept the things for which no explanation is really adequate and put together something in the end that is really satisfying. The only kinds of people that put together answers that satisfy them are the various varieties of true believers.

We must constantly look for the complexities. Here we have some manageable, hard facts such as facts of geography, resources, populations, trade, production, and weaponry, and we have a whole mass of soft facts, which are made up of all those things that float around in people's heads and are also decisive in their behavior. We strive and struggle to understand them, but I think that along with a new and brilliant generation of social scientists who are going to arrive at all these satisfying formulas, we ought to also raise a new generation of novelist who will convey to us some of the other aspects of the truth.

In terms of how useful the generational explanation is as compared to other types of explanations such as ethnic or racial explanations, I can only say that we can only pose a question like that in relation to a concrete situation. We have to go in and, to the best of our capacity, see how we can learn what the relative weights and places of these different elements in the situation might be.

Field:

I have three observations, First, this chapter seemed to emphasize the importance of direct experience as conditioning one's world view. This runs against the literature on political socialization that argues that one's inheritance was at least equally as important as one's experience in shaping one's outlook. What is learned first is most durable in one's basic orientation toward politics.

Secondly, the remarks have a sadly deterministic quality. The eminent elites who had produced the independence miracle are now gone, and their societies have gone down the road. There is an element of a paradise lost here. But we might turn that around. In spite of these very striking changes, there are also some dramatic continuities. We might say that even the major changes that we have seen in India in the last three months may ultimately loom less significant than some enduring qualities.

Finally, I think that in contrasting those nationalist leaders with their sons and daughters, you are consumed with imagery. I think that you have blown up these persons and you bestow on them the heroic qualities of the events in which they have participated. Thus, you are almost implicitly denigrating their successors as the faceless lot that would have to face the more mundane tasks of presiding over the young state.

Isaacs:

I should point out that I only spoke of the idealized values that the nationalist leaders strove for. I was not speaking of idealized achievements at all. I don't know by what stretch of the imagination one could speak of the Philippines and India, of anything that was lost there, as a paradise. This would take a degree of departure from sober reality that even I in my most novelistic flights would never be guilty of.

5

The Concept of Generations in Military Institutions: Brazil and Peru Compared

Alfred C. Stepan

Brazil in 1964 and Peru in 1968 witnessed boundary changes in their patterns of civil-military relations and in the nature of their socioeconomic systems. Before exploring the possible role that generational effects played in these changes, we must briefly place the concept of generation within the contextual setting of military institutions.

When talking about the military, we can usefully begin by directing attention to something to which the military themselves pay overwhelming attention: their corporate survival and institutional integrity. However, if we want to analyze the emergence of a new military-led political design, we also need to examine the interaction between the military as a corporate institution and the domestic and international environment that may contribute to the changes in this new institutional model—that is, one must examine the conditions that are either resistive or supportive to the installation of the military's new design.

We need two further caveats. The first caveat is that patron-client vertical relations, not merely horizontal age cohorts, are a frequent characteristic of military generations; thus, we cannot be too age-bound when we talk of a generation in the military. For example, there may be a special tactical group within the military in which captains through generals are affected by a particular experience. We can talk about it as a generational experience, but we are not talking about a narrow *age cohort*, but of an *experiencial cohort* within which the members' age span will often be as broad as twenty-five years.

The second caveat concerns the fact that military institutions are characterized by bureaucratic routines, doctrines, and intense formal socialization systems via the military schools. In the larger countries of Latin America this is even more marked than in the developed countries. The amount of time that one is likely to spend in military schools in a major Latin American army is about twice as long as in a French or North American Army. The General Staff Schools are frequently three years long in Latin America, while in the United States they are nine months long. So we are speaking of institutions that have some socialization capacity, where people are selected in and selected out partly on the basis of how they perform ideologically within such schooling systems. Given this socialization process, we might call a particular cohort experience a generational experience, but this is going to have a more enduring institutional impact if it is integrated into doctrine and then passed on in the military schooling system to those who did not share the initial cohort experience.

Thus, if a complex corporate institution like the military undergoes a shift in its political behavior, as in the cases of Brazil and Peru, we should, in examining the generational hypothesis, of course follow the standard practice in generational studies of determining whether there has been a significant shift in recruitment patterns. But we must also look for the presence or absence of profound cohort experiences and we should explore any changes in the internal and external environments. These changes might result in a new perception of threat to the military, which in turn may lead to a new definition by the institution of its mission and capacity in relation to a civil society.

Let me now discuss some of these ideas in the context of Brazil and Peru.[a] On the question of the bases of recruitment, we find that there is no observable change in recruitment patterns in either country from the period before to the period after the boundary changes. The great difference in the content between the Brazilian model and the Peruvian model cannot be explained in terms of socioeconomic origin. Officers are recruited from virtually identical social strata before and after the changes. Figures do show that in the last forty years there have generally been fewer upper-class officers (because there have been more opportunities in civilian society) and, contrary to most empirical findings, less lower-class recruitment. Professionalization of the military has meant that it has become less accessible for those without at least a high school education. So, a more homogenous, middle-class basis of recruitment is to be found in both cases.

But this is obviously not going to help us explain why Brazil is basically a rightest exclusionary regime and why Peru, while authoritarian, is an inclusionary regime that has carried out some of the most important structural changes of any regime in Latin American history. Having explored— and for these cases rejected—the explanatory power of new or different recruitment processes, let us now explore the experiential cohort hypothesis.

In Brazil I did uncover an attitudinal pattern that is traceable to an intense cohort experience. This experience appeared to have had an independent impact in shaping a political generation within the military. Here I have in mind Mannheim's (1928) idea that a political generation is characterized by shared common experiences that lead to characteristic modes of thought in both attitudes and collective strivings.

I uncovered this Brazilian cohort experience in doing aggregate analysis of the careers of the entire universe of generals in active duty in 1964. The biographical data was excellent for all 102 of these officers. But for political analysis, analysis of the entire universe is not as politically meaningful as the analysis of subgroups within the universe. I wanted to have some idea who was the core group behind the coup. I identified this core group by means of structured interviews. Of the ten generals who emerged as members of the core group, I found that five of the ten had participated in World War II, all had been on the permanent staff of the Escola Superior de Guerra, all had attended

---

[a]The data to support what follows is drawn from field research in both countries, much of which is reported in Stepan (1971, 1973, and forthcoming).

foreign schools, and all had graduated number one in a major army school. Of the remainder of the universe, only one out of ninety-two had done all five things. The statistical probability of such a difference occurring by chance alone is one in a thousand. However, the fact that I had a statistically significant finding did not explain what the connection was among these variables. In tracing this out, I found that prior experience of participation in World War II seemed extremely important.

In conducting interviews with these generals, I asked, "What did participation in World War II mean to you?" I should note here that we are talking about the only military group in all of Latin America that participated in ground combat in the war, and we are also talking about a group that eventually received the surrender of a German division. The interviews again and again tapped common perceptions and themes. One comment was that they had had a terrific nationalist sendoff involving great parades. When they got to Italy, however, they found that their uniforms looked like those of the enemy; they also found that their supplies were slow in coming. They were in fact humiliated in their first encounter in Italy. The German forces cut right through them and inflicted great losses on the American flank. There was then the recognition that they were simply not up to world standards, and thus they fell back to reserve status. In these interviews the generals speak of their embarrassment, of their kidding themselves that they were a world class military unit; yet also there was proud recognition of the fact that in the process of serious competition, they quickly achieved world level standards. This too provided them with a jaundiced view of politicians who talk of nationalism but cannot deliver. This is the way in which they came to see persons like Mussolini and Goulart as those who could verbalize power but not realize it.

The second point to emerge from these interviews was that these generals had very favorable feelings toward the United States, and this is somewhat atypical in relation to the rest of the Brazilian military. They felt that they had come out of that apprenticeship as a better army and had soon arrived at a higher level of autonomy. They also felt that the capitalist model of production and the formal democratic system had been consistent with the U.S. military's achieving world power status. They felt that Brazil could become a world power via the process of integration and competition with capitalist countries such as the United States. Their model of Brazilian nationalism was thus one that entailed internationalism, capitalism, and competitive apolitical efficiency. Most military organizations do not approach nationalism in these terms and for a variety of organizational and ideological reasons are more ambivalent about capitalism.

I could see how these ideas were congruent with what they did in 1964. Yet it was difficult to say what exactly was the connection between what happened in 1944 and what happened twenty years later. This, I believed, was simply too long a jump without some institutional nexus. So, the next thing I looked for was a link between the Escola Superior de Guerra and the World War II experience. The obvious place to start was by speaking to the founder of the General War College, which had been the first of its kind in Latin America. He suggested that there was the desire to institutionalize the learning experiences of World War II. They built this into the schooling system, and thus it passed from generation to generation. This, then, was the institutional nexus that carried these men to their emergence as national leaders. They imposed much of their model in 1964.

Implicit in my discussion of the central role of professional military schools in a setting such as Brazil's is a conception of a "new professionalism" that plays a major role in forging a new "institutional generation" within the military. This conception of military professionalism is quite different from that of the "classic professionalism" so clearly and forcefully articulated in Huntington's (1957) *The Soldier and the State*. Here I should underscore that it is not so much that we disagree but that we are talking about two completely different models of military professionalism. In most key characteristics the two professionalisms are diametrically opposed. The core assumption of what I call his model of "classic professionalism" is that the dominant function of the military is external defense. In the "new professional" model it is my assumption that it is internal security that is actually perceived as the dominant function of the military. In the old professional model, it is taken as given that civilians accept the legitimacy of government, while my view is that in most Third World countries the governments take as given the fact that some segments of society will challenge the legitimacy of the regime. In the classic professionalism model, the military possess highly specialized skills that are incompatible with civilians' political skills. In the new professionalism, civilian and military skills are seen as highly interrelated. In classic professionalism, the scope of military professional action becomes increasingly restricted. In new professionalism, the scope becomes increasingly unrestricted. In the classic model, the impact of professional socialization renders the military politically neutral, whereas in the new professionalism it renders the military highly politicized. In what I see as the new professionalism, which I argue is becoming the modal pattern throughout the developing world, this politicization contributes to military political managerialism and role expansion.

This new professionalism was built into the Brazilian military, and the definition of the threat to the army was then seen through the lenses of the new professionalism. So too, the definition of what Brazil needed to become great was seen through these same lenses. Evidence for this comes through a comparison of the curriculum of the General Staff School in 1956 and in 1966. In 1956 there were no classes on counterguerrilla warfare, none on the linkage between internal security and national security, and virtually nothing on communism. By 1966, there were over two-hundred hours on internal security, over one-hundred on irregular warfare, and only twenty-four hours on the topic of territorial warfare.

In the years leading up to 1964 there were major changes in the political, social, and economic environment that the new professionals saw as profoundly threatening. Within this context of perceived crisis the original political cohort, now institutionally strengthened because many other officers had been socialized into their doctrine, felt that they had forged an ideology, a program, and a new professional cadre that put it in a better position than civilian politicians to respond to what they saw as the corporate and national crisis they faced. Thus we witnessed a boundary change from the old model of civil-military relations to direct military rule.

The Brazilian boundary change thus entailed three elements relevant for our discussion: an initial generational cohort experience (1942-1945), a subsequent formation of new professional institutional generation (1950-1960), and a final crisis intensification (1961-1964) that culminated (1964) with the new professionals assuming power under the direction of the initial experiential cohort. Thus, while the concept of generation is useful for the analysis of the boundary change in Brazil, we need to distinguish between, and to use, both the concept of an "experiential cohort generation" and a "new professional institutional generation." But these concepts alone are not sufficient to explain the boundary change without the idea of the military's perception of an intense crisis.

What about the Peruvian military? In my research I have not found anything like the World War II generational cohort that I found in Brazil. However I did find new professionalism, a new professionalism so strong that one might say that it forged a new "institutional generation." When this new institutional generation perceived that it was confronted with an intense corporate and national threat it too effected a boundary change in civil-military relations by seizing power and attempting to impose a new military-directed political and economic model on the country. Despite these similarities with Brazil, it is obvious that the content and consequences of new professionalism have been sharply different in Peru than in Brazil. The post-1968 Peruvian military, in complete contradiction to Brazil, became one of the Third World leaders in the search for new forms in which to use the power of the state to control multinational corporations. It carried out a more sweeping agrarian reform than any Latin American country besides Cuba, and it initiated a series of experiments in new forms of worker-ownership and participation.

What was the content of new professionalism in Peru and why did the new professional generation react to their perception of intense threat in such a sharply different way than the Brazilian new professionals? In doing my research on Peru I wanted to explore the origins of this new military style and to further examine my new professionalism hypothesis. I took a look at the content of the articles written by the Peruvian military in their journals. I created eight different categories by which to code the articles. For the purposes of this chapter, I can collapse two of these categories into one, namely, internal war and engineering social change, and sociopolitical analysis. In 1954-1957 only 1.7 percent of all the articles fell in that collapsed category that I would now call new professionalism. In 1963–1965, by contrast, over 50 percent of the articles fell into that category. In other words, after the Algerian war, after the Cuban revolution, after the U.S. exportation of the counterinsurgency doctrine, and after major peasant invasions and uprisings frightened the Peruvian military, they began to focus on the nexus between internal security and national development. The new professional military socialization emerged, but its content was very different in Peru than it was in Brazil. The nature of the threat as defined by the Peruvian military was quite different. The nature of the solution for the country was likewise presented as quite different in these articles.

My content analysis shows that for an eight- to ten-year period before the assumption of power, the military had been undergoing a profound redefinition of its mission. By 1961 they had begun to create a series of nonissues within the military institution. By nonissues I mean things that they considered absolutely had to be done and that there would be no argument about. So the creation of institutional nonissues on things that are potentially highly explosive is an important ingredient. Land reform was made a nonissue by 1962. It was judged that Peru was a country where the oligarchy owned too much land, where there was unrest, where there was an unjust social system, and that this constituted a security threat due to the marginalization of much of the Peruvian population. It terrified the military to find that some of 80 percent of the Peruvians in the Sierra did not identify with the Peruvian nation. A second nonissue concerned the view that Peru should have greater control of its raw materials, especially via the expropriation of IPC. By 1964, then, there was a clear diagnosis that social change was essential in order to prevent a revolution in which the military would be the major losers. Thus, four years before the military actually assumed power we can say that the Peruvian army as a corporate unit had already undergone a ten-year institutional transformation. They had redefined their mission, their threats, their preferred security policies, and they felt they had expanded their sociopolitical capacity to direct change. In this loose sense then we can speak of a new Peruvian institutional army generation by as early as 1964.

I underscore the fact that a new institutional perspective existed by 1964 because this prior socialization and prior definition of corporate threats profoundly shaped how they responded to the guerrilla uprising that broke out in 1965. By 1964 the military journals were predicting that fundamental structural change was necessary to avoid a revolution. Even though the actual size of the guerrilla units were relatively small, they tied the Peruvian military up in knots for almost a year. Although they defeated the guerrillas, this threat intensified their desire for structural change and their dislike of having to perform the role of being the watchdogs of the oligarchy. Their new professional diagnosis was that if there was no structural change, there would eventually be an even stronger guerrilla movement. And, if the guerrillas won, the watchdog military would be the first to be eliminated by the successful revolutionary forces.

By 1968 the Belaúnde government's total inability to act on either agrarian reform or IPC nationalization convinced key army leaders that the only way to achieve structural change was to seize power and impose it themselves. So, as in Brazil, in Peru the new professionalism, when combined with the perception of corporate and national threat, lead to a boundary change. But in Peru the definition of the enemies and the definition of the solutions was quite different.

So far we have explained why, unlike the Brazilian military, the Peruvian military attempted to restabilize the political system by policies of structural change and economic nationalism. But to understand the content of the Peruvian new professional's nationalism we must see how the internal military generational shift intersected with, and was reinforced by, a paradigm shift in the definition of the nature of the development predicament brought about by a new generation of Latin American social theorists, the *dependencia* school.

In the early 1950s Raúl Prebisch and ECLA formulated a Latin American nationalist development paradigm that was not challenged effectively until the mid-to-late 1960s. The Prebisch thesis was that there was a permanent deterioration in the terms of trade for poorer countries that exported raw materials and food stuffs in exchange for industrialized goods. Their proposed solution was industrialization—the manufacture of these goods in Latin America. That became the definition of a progressive response, the very definition of nationalism. By the mid-1960s more and more social scientists began to look at the results of these import substitution policies. It became obvious that there was development behind a very high tariff wall, and it became increasingly obvious that some countries had been so interested in industrialization that they had given what amounted to subsidies and special import quotas to foreign multinationals. Not much attention was paid to whether or not transfer pricing mechanisms within these firms were adversely affecting the host economies. It also became apparent to many that much of the funds of these firms were being raised locally. In addition, the assumption had been made in the initial model that the host countries would receive technology, as well as some export earnings. It turns out, in the case of Peru, that in over 50 percent of the contracts there was the prohibition of exports if any patented technology was employed. In essence, the import substitution strategy for development had built an industrial structure with a very high import coefficient, with very little potential for export; it had raised domestic prices, and it had not brought about the transfer of technology. The Peruvian military was first to build the *dependencia* critique of the ECLA model into their military schooling system. If we look at other reformist regimes in Latin America (i.e., Cárdenas, Perón, or Vargas), the definition of nationalism was much more restricted than that one now being applied by Peru.

This *dependencia* perspective helped shape the Peruvian regime's geopolitical world view as well. They saw Peru as a small country with little power, and they recognized the need for Andean Pact unity. The most important security struggles were seen not as being between East and West, as Brazil thought, but between North and South. To be able to negotiate effectively with the industrialized powers, Peru saw no alternative but to expand its factors of power by uniting with other Third World countries. A crucial factor in negotiating with the multinationals is the size of the market. If Peru can mold the Andean Pact, this becomes an attractive market. Only then can Peru have the power to tighten the restrictions for entry. The point is not to block off foreign capital, but to establish a principle of nonautomatic entry. To the extent that this would now be a larger market, Peru could give a degree of monopoly entrance, and be in a stronger position to bargain over the terms of entry. So it is not a simple nationalism that bars entry, but a very complex package of post*dependencia* policy programs.

Let me conclude with a few brief observations about the utilization of the concept of generations when thinking about the military. I would say that to some extent the new professional aspect of military generations can be viewed as an independent variable. For example, shortly after the Peruvian experiment started, the Torres government in Bolivia announced that they would emulate Peru. But in the total absence of any prior development of a programmatic consensus within the military institution, they split almost immediately. We must understand that an integral part of the Peruvian model is this prior eight- to ten-year programmatic consensus. However, we must also be aware that an initial new professional doctrinal consensus over "nonissues," while a great aid in implementing the first round of changes, is not a substitute for a political organization with a strong capacity to formulate solutions for new problems and to build an enduring political constituency for the new regime. The lack of such a capacity contributed to the political and economic crises the Peruvian new professionals began to encounter by 1975.

One final point: Actions as well as doctrines can create a military generation. The massive repression and torture imposed by the Chilean military has become an independent factor in creating a military generation. Even if the members wanted to extricate from power, they must face the institutional and personal reprisals that face them.

Discussion

Huntington:

You mentioned two things relative to the process of the forming of a generation in the military. One was the shared experiences of officers. The other was the process you described in the context of Peru, although not quite the same way in connection with Brazil, of consensus building, or the decisions made concerning what were the nonissues and the way in which they became almost a state of mind within the military establishment. My first question concerns whether or not you see the guerrilla campaign in Peru in the mid-1960s as having the same function as the Brazilian officers' experience in Italy in World War II. This is a common way of thinking about generations—that is, in terms of the impact of a shared traumatic experience upon people of roughly the same age. If these are comparable, why in Brazil didn't the World War II experience of both humiliation and competence building produce a 1964 in 1950?

Secondly, in relation to your distinction between the "old" professionalism and the "new" professionalism, do you see any evidence of generational differences within Peru or Brazil? Do you see, for instance, any tension between the majors and the colonels versus the generals?

Stepan:

Because it started ten years ago, everyone who reached the rank of general in Peru, was more or less a "new" professional. Latin American coups, unlike African or Asian coups, are generals' coups. They are manifested in a very institutional way. As to the question as to why there was such a long wait for the impact of the shared experience, I think that in the case of Brazil but not in Peru, we can point to the acceptance of the idea by the World War II political cohort that a major power is one that in some ways has liberal political institutions. Despite over a decade of authoritarian rule, Brazil still has parties, still has elections, and still has a Congress. We must remember that the World War II cohort was sent off by a corporatist and was defeated a corporatist in Mussolini. Their preferred choice was to socialize the civilians to understand the realities of national politics as they saw them. That is why within three years of the establishment of the General War College over 50 percent of all the students who went to it were civilians. They didn't want to assume power themselves, they wanted to identify key civilians, not just from the government, but from the press, the church, and other civilian institutions. They wanted to socialize a new civilian generation into their perspective of the model Brazil would have to follow. They hoped that the political elite could do it themselves, backed by them. When they discerned that the political elite could not handle it, they assumed power. Since there had been this liberal element, it meant that they didn't fully specify the nonissues to the extent that they had been specified in Peru.

Field:

I'd like to return to some of your earlier comments concerning the 1964 coup in Brazil. You seem to have emphasized the socializing impact of the World War

II experience. Others have explained the events of 1964 in terms of the ferment in the countryside, or the mobilization of the peasantry by almost every conceivable radical faction. To what extent do you feel that the critical socialization experience of the military has been internal to the military and its privileged position in the society at large, and to what extent do you think their perceptions of their role are conditioned by the changes in the society of which they are partially a part?

Stepan:

I look at military institutions in much the same way in which I look at the church. To some extent they are both *situational* elites as much as class elites. The military elites are elites that get much of their privileges from being members of a stable state and from carrying out specific functions within the state. The extent to which they see the state structure as becoming fragile threatens their positions as a *situational* elite. The diagnosis of what tasks may be necessary to reconstitute a stable society—tasks undertaken by both the Peruvian and the Brazilian militaries—will differ in each society. The Brazilian military defined much of the problem as coming from populist politicians and labor leaders. In Peru the definition of what was involved in a reequilibriation of the system entailed the elimination of one sector of the oligarchy, the rural land owners, as well as a more nationalist policy. In both cases the military as an institution felt threatened, although Peru is at a much lower level of development than Brazil. That is why I speak of inclusionary corporatist responses and exclusionary corporatist responses. Both of them were responses to radicalism. However, the military's solution on how to resolve radicalism, to put it in a containable form, took the shape of an inclusionary corporatist response in Peru that has much more in common with Cárdenas, with Perón, and with Vargas. The exclusionary response in Brazil has a lot more to do with the exhaustion of the first stage of import substitution. The inflation rates of Argentina, Chile, and Brazil before the exclusionary coups were extremely high. Strike levels were very high; the ratio of debt service to total exports was over twenty percent for all countries. Peru's inflation and debt figures were lower, and so too was its strike level. In Peru every indicator of conflict and structural tension was lower except for the indicator of peasant mobilization. In other words, there are different sets of indicators that are important. While Peru is an inclusionary corporatist response, Brazil is in a family with Argentina and Chile as exclusionary corporatist responses. The first act in such systems is the exclusion of the politically relevant working class sectors.

McCann:

I've recently had the chance to go back and look at the constitutional role of the World War II Brazilian military, and it was a rather revealing experience. I came to the conclusion that there was a tension in Brazilian ideology, or mission, between what was the supposed role of the army according to the Imperial

Constitution, where it was specified that the army was to defend the country against foreign enemies, and its actual activities. The Constitution of 1891 added something very interesting. It spoke of internal control as being one of the missions of the army. It seems to me that in looking at the years down to 1964 there was a constant play back and forth between groups in the army that saw the principal mission of the army as being external and groups that saw it as being internal. If we take a look at the people who went through the military school between 1902 through 1915, we can see most were very anxious to have a European-style army. If we look at what the army was really doing all through this period, and later, we find them fighting no wars. What we find is a whole series of internal involvements by the military in Brazil. Yet there was a professionalization process going on as well in that they were becoming more like a European army. But they were being called upon to use that military power internally. I also wonder if in some way the experiences of the 1920s and the 1930s had a kind of psychological and intellectual effect on the Brazilian military that the 1965 experience in the mountains had on the Peruvian military.

Stepan:

I, of course, never made the claim that Brazil was an "old" professional army before World War II. I agree with you that the three constitutional clauses were built in by civilian elites so that the military always had some political role. They did have an obligation to obey the president within the limits of the law and to maintain internal order. Discretionary obedience was built in by the political leaders as a constraint on the executive. In my first book (Stepan 1971), I referred to this as the moderator model and I argued that it accurately described the pattern of civil-military relations in Brazil for much of the period from the fall of the monarchy until 1964. Thus I am not assuming for a second that Brazil had a classic "old" professional model before 1964. What I was trying to capture was the difference between a military that performs a moderator function before 1964 and a military that rules with its own program after 1964.

In this sense I think that there was a profound difference between pre- and post-1964. In interview after interview it was reported to me by generals that before they developed their new schooling system they didn't feel competent to define a political project by themselves. The intellectual and social domination of the civilian elites was equally as strong in the Peruvian case. This was a part of the boundary maintenance within the moderator model that is broken down by an army which no longer believes that the civilian elites are capable of handling the situation but believes that their new professionalism has given them the capacity to rule.

Dominguez:

I am going to try to formulate my question in explicitly generational terms— that is, it seemed to me that you were talking in both cases not about one crucial formative event, but really about two at least. In each case the first formative event was an external event. The Brazilian experience in World War II was a directly experienced external event. The Peruvian external event was imported; they imported counterinsurgency doctrines. The importance of both of those events is that they led to the formation or to the reshaping of military institutions. The efforts were then directed to the maintaining of the ideas of the formative generation over a longer period of time.

The second formative event with an impact on these military generations occurred in Peru with the experience of repressing the 1965 insurgency, and occurred in Brazil with the Goulart government's having to face up to internal events. Thus we can come to think of this generation as having had two major formative events, one being the move toward consensus building and institutional formation, and the second leading to the kind of action that you are analyzing in your study. So do you think that in forming generations and in leading them to action that not one, but more than one, formative experience is needed?

Secondly, I am led to wonder what the conflict might be between a generational explanation and an institutional explanation. If an institution tries to standardize opinions and behavior across generations and if a generational explanation in its pure form can conceive of changes from one generation to the next, then the argument that I just made about formative generations building institutions comes into conflict with this sort of explanation.

The final point concerns whether you see other aspects that could be associated with the generational hypothesis in Peru and Brazil. For instance, the Brazilian generational hypothesis begins in the mid-1940s. Now as these persons grow old, can one say something about the stages in the life cycle at the time that these events happened that would tell us something different from what we might learn through the use of cohort analysis? Can this be done for Peru? Can one say something about transgenerational alliances? In Peru and Brazil we've observed generals' coups. Are there varieties of support for these generals within the armed forces that have generational characteristics? Do you have the generals and the lieutenants versus the colonels? Or do you have fully institutional coups with unified commands?

Stepan:

All of what you say is reasonable. My point here is that we are dealing with a complex institution. Cohort experiences have to be filtered through a formal ideology, and then passed by the socialization process. So I've never accepted the generational hypothesis in its pure form for so extremely complex an institution. I emphasize doctrinal formulation and then incorporation. If that's absent, then complex institutions like the military or like the church have a characteristic way of handling troublesome generations—they are merely defined out of the institution itself. Most of the radical Catholic generation has no institutional impact after a while, because they are outside the institution. That is why I stress the linkage between generational experience and institutional expression in ideology.

I like the idea of looking at multiple formative experiences. Instead of a simple one step generational experience there is probably often something like a complex three step sequence: a major challenge, an institutional response, and then another challenge that in some way the political system seems incapable of responding to, and the military responds in the place of the civilians.

I emphasize that to be successful, an experiential cohort must integrate its subgroup experience into the entire group's routine program of doctrinal socialization. However, it is obvious that this socialization process never completely succeeds and no military organization is an ideological monolith or behaves as a unitary actor. There is thus some predictable variation. For example, the core group of Brazilian generals in 1964 had as a distant end goal some form of liberal political institutions. There was a generational difference. By and large the captains, the majors, and the lieutenants did not share this interest in liberal institutions. Many of the young officers wanted more sweeping reforms and less liberalism. They wanted more authoritarianism, they wanted to close Congress, they wanted to constrict elections more tightly. That is why the Peruvian model, which began in 1968 before the Brazilian "economic miracle" had begun, created great tension in Brazil in 1968 to 1969. Some of the younger Brazilian officers watched Peru and thought that it looked like a model to which they could relate. It was a more purely military model.

In Peru it seems to me that the passion that the senior officers leading the process bring to their discourse is much more intense than it is at the general staff and military schooling levels. There is a routinization of the goals of the Peruvian revolutionary government. There appears to be no significant military group to the left of the current government leaders. If the economic and political pressure keeps building up on the military government, the tendency will be to consolidate, rather than to expand, the original core program of the new professionals.

Hopkins:

If you look at the question of generational change, you could look at group level or macroanalysis, and this seems to be largely what you have been doing in terms of the military. On the other hand, you could think of individual-level explanations—the impact of one or a few individuals on a system, for example. In this way you could apply generational analysis to regimes that could not be characterized as either "new" or "old" professional. To what extent can you see in Latin America this kind of analytic distinction?

Stepan:

There is always room for some individual-level analysis, but I like to put it in the context of the level of development of a society and in the context of the class and institutional formation of that society. In this sense we could say that the conditions that Cárdenas inherited in late 1934 in Mexico were very favorable to an inclusionary attempt. He was a brilliant politician. He utilized and expanded the available space where a very poor politician could have failed to capitalize on the opportunity.

Yet, the greatest politician in the world could not have turned postcoup Chile in 1973 or postcoup Argentina in 1966 into an inclusionary regime with the wide, Gramcian-like hegemony in civil society of the type that developed in Mexico. So, there is room for the role of the individual in political analysis, but it has to be bounded by some analysis of the social dynamics, economic constraints, and group politics of a given situation.

References

Huntington, Samuel P. 1957. *The Soldier and the State: The Theory and Politics of Civil-Military Relations.* Cambridge, Mass.: Harvard University Press.

Mannheim, Karl. 1928. *Essays on the Sociology of Knowledge.* London: Routledge and Kegan Paul.

Stephan, Alfred C. 1971. *The Military in Politics: Changing Patterns in Brazil.* Princeton, N.J.: Princeton University Press.

———. 1973. "The New Professionalism of Internal Warfare and Military Role Expansion." In Alfred C. Stepan, (ed.), *Authoritarian Brazil: Origins, Policies, and Future.* New Haven, Conn.: Yale University Press.

———. Forthcoming. *The State and Society: Peru in Comparative Perspective.* Princeton, N.J.: Princeton University Press.

Motilal, Jawaharlal, Indira, and Sanjay in India's Political Transformation

Myron Weiner

Since we are concerned with the topic of political generations, these remarks on the current Indian scene must be tailored to fit the cloth of generational change. In fact, doing so is not too constraining, for we can begin this discussion of India's institutional transformation by noting that Indira Gandhi's decision to turn against India's founding fathers by suspending India's democratic institutions has a special poignancy when we recall that her father and grandfather played such a central role in creating and strengthening those institutions. The story of India's first Indian-dominated constitutional convention is of particular interest, for it not only throws light on the role played by Indira Gandhi's grandfather, but it also tells us a great deal about the contrasting uses of power by Nehru and by his daughter, Indira.

In 1928 the Congress Party appointed an all-party Constitutional Reform Committee, chaired by Motilal Nehru, then President of the Congress Party. Congress appointed the Committee to protest the decision by the British to send a British delegation led by Sir John Simon to review the workings of the 1919 Reform Act and to devise a new constitutional structure for India. The Indian nationalists took offense at the Simon delegation on the grounds that it contained no Indian members. Thus, for the first time, the Indian nationalists created their own commission to explore the question of constitutional reform. The Indian Constitutional Reform Committee, under Motilal Nehru, produced a draft constitution that provided for a declaration of human rights, a parliamentary form of government, a bicameral legislature, adult suffrage, federalism, a redrawing of provincial boundaries along linguistic lines, and an independent judiciary. The committee report was a formal assertion by a group of educated Indians that an independent India would be based on the Westminster model of parliamentary government, with some modifications to suit the regional diversity of India.

The committee report was controversial, not for these provisions, but for its rejection of proposals for communal electorates that would have given separate voting status for Muslims and other minorities. But there was even more controversy over its call for dominion status rather than independence for India.

Opposition to the report was led by Jawaharlal Nehru, the son of Motilal. Jawaharlal took the position that it was too late to call for dominion status for India, that India had to become an independent nation. As the controversy became bitter, Gandhi sought to bring father and son together with a proposal that Congress accept the Motilal Nehru report with the proviso that if the British did not accept the report within one year, the Indian National Congress would then lead a mass movement for independence. With that condition, Jawaharlal Nehru accepted the compromise and the following year (1929) he was elected president of the all-India National Congress, as successor to his father. When it became clear within a few months that the British had not accepted the report, Gandhi launched the famous salt march, and in 1930 Congress passed the resolution demanding independence from Britain.

The historical account highlights the tension between father and son as well as draws our attention to the role payed by Nehru's father in drafting proposals for the institutional structure that Jawaharlal was later to work. Although Jawaharlal proved to be politically independent of his father, the father's ideas about democratic and parliamentary institutions were enduring influences on the son. In contrast, Indira Gandhi was a dutiful daughter, never publicly (or, as far as we know, privately) disagreeing with her father, but we know now, in retrospect, that she did not share her father's commitment to democratic institutions.

How has Mrs. Gandhi sought to revise the institutions created by India's founding fathers and for what reason? These are the issues I should like to discuss.

Among the elements that made up India's democratic system were an independent judiciary, a free press, and competitive open elections. Accompanying these institutions was a dominant Congress Party that contained a large number of dissident factions that allied themselves with dissident factions in the opposition parties, thereby creating a constant interplay between the governing Congress Party and the opposition. This was the party system that operated at both the state and national levels. The system provided for a high level of organized political participation at the local level, through a large number of local elections for village *panchayats* and district councils, up to state assemblies and the national parliament. Electoral participation rates were remarkably high for a poor and largely illiterate country and were even higher in local than in national elections. This system was also built around a powerful administrative structure with considerable autonomy, but which was nonetheless limited by a large number of organized political groups that restrained the exercise of bureaucratic power. The political system was, compared with most developing countries, an open one with high turnover in political leadership, especially in the states, but even in the central government.

Its weaknesses have been much discussed. It was a highly accommodating system able to cope with enormous societal conflicts. But it was not a particularly innovative system in its management of economic policies. The system gave a great deal of power to individuals at the local level who were often able to impede the carrying out of national policies. Many policies in the areas of agriculture, land reform, and taxation advocated by the national government were not implemented at the state level. The system also placed considerable restraint on the functioning of the private sector. Private sector expansion was restrained by enormous bureaucratic regulations. The antibusiness attitudes of many of India's political leaders, couched in terms of socialism, tended to reinforce bureaucratic authority. The bureaucracy created inordinate delays in the carrying out of many economic policies and national-level decisions, particularly those that related to the private sector's efforts to import machinery, obtain licenses, and expand investment.

During the past few years efforts were made to centralize authority, to move power from the states to the center and from the political elites to the bureaucracy. The declaration of an "Emergency" in June 1975 was the culmination of these steps, though it is important to note that the trend toward greater centralism preceded the move toward authoritarianism. Mrs. Gandhi declared a "National Emergency," arrested opposition leaders (except for the pro-Soviet communist who supported her), banned twenty-six political organizations, and restricted the press. In the months that followed, the government tightened its control over the press and in effect prevented the opposition from reaching India's reading public. Three institutions were singled out for attack by the government: the opposition, the press, and the judiciary. More striking, however, was Mrs. Gandhi's attack at her own Congress Party.

In some respects this attack against Congress preceded the declaration of the "Emergency." In 1969, just two years after the 1967 elections, in which Mrs. Gandhi's party won a close majority in the parliament while losing control over about half of the state governments, Mrs. Gandhi found herself at odds with the state Congress Party bosses. This clash came to a head in 1969 when the president of India died and a contest ensued for choosing his successor. The Congress Party leadership, over Mrs. Gandhi's objections, chose Sanjiva Reddy, a man who had been part of the inner core of politicians that had played a role in dominating the politics of the country during the previous decade. Mrs. Gandhi obviously feared that his election as President of India would be a threat to her, for she would have recognized that in the next few years, if the Congress Party continued its decline, the president would be in a powerful position to exercise influence over who would serve as prime minister. She soon began quietly to seek ways to undercut his election and ultimately she backed the candidate of the opposition party. With support from dissident elements of her own party, Mrs. Gandhi succeeded in getting the candidate of the opposition to win the election. That represented a breakdown in the cohesion in the Congress Party and led some Congress leaders to seriously consider taking disciplinary action against their own prime minister. I won't go into the details of the political struggle that then took place, except to say that after an initial reconciliation, Congress split in two, with some state chief ministers siding with Mrs. Gandhi's wing of the party and with some supporting her opponents. She called national parliamentary elections in 1971, and in spite of a weak party organization under her control, she effectively mounted an impressive national campaign that brought her wing of the party to victory. In some respects it was more of a presidential-type than parliamentary election with the victorious Congress centering around a single figure.

In the next few years Mrs. Gandhi succeeded in eliminating not only the state chief ministers who had opposed her, but even those who had sided with her. Similarly, she eroded the position of each of the remaining state party bosses. She made it very clear that she did not want any political figures in the country to have any independent popular or organizational sources of power. The result was that she was left with a Congress Party organization with no effective power base in the states. Each state party organization was headed by appointees of Mrs. Gandhi and each of the chief ministers was loyal to her. What emerged was not only a more centralized party whose state leaders were dependent upon the center, but a new restructuring of the federal system itself, for with a weakening of the party, governmental power became more centralized. In those few instances where state chief ministers tried to build an independent power base, she quickly dismissed them. Most recently, even after the "National Emergency," she dismissed the politically powerful Chief Minister of Uttar Pradesh. In short, one major institutional change was the weakening of the Congress Party state organizations, and with it, the weakening of the power of the chief ministers.

A second major institutional change effected by Mrs. Gandhi was the strengthening of the intelligence apparatus of the central government. It soon became clear that as the local Congress Party became decreasingly effective, the local party was less and less able to keep the central government apprised of the issues and conflicts extant at the local level. This necessitated the expansion of an independent central intelligence organization. In the Prime Minister's Secretariat there is a unit known as the Research and Analysis Wing (RAW), which is widely seen in India as an effective intelligence-gathering organization. A critical feature of this particular intelligence unit is that it is located in the Prime Minister's Secretariat and that it reports directly to the prime minister. People to whom I have spoken have reported that RAW has compiled dossiers on the opposition, on dissidents within Congress, and even on senior Congress officials. RAW was an important instrument for making possible the implementation of the "Emergency" on the night of June 26, 1975, when thousands of persons were rounded up at their places of residence in an operation that required an extremely efficient intelligence apparatus.

A third institutional development was the expansion of the paramilitary police forces. These include the Border Security Forces, a unit of approximately 100,000 persons, the Central Reserve Police, and the Home Guards, with a combined strength of roughly half a million men. A critical feature of these agencies is that they are not part of the military, and hence not under the control of the Defense Ministry. Nor are they under the control of the state governments, as are the state police. The paramilitary forces are directly under the control of the Home Ministry. This means that the prime minister has control of a quasimilitary force for dealing with domestic crises. It was therefore possible to carry out the "Emergency" without using the army. There is no reason to believe that the military is not politically dependable, although it is interesting to note that a major justification for the "Emergency" was that the opposition parties, and Jayaprakash Narayan, its central figure, had called for disaffection within the army. But the use of these paramilitary forces tends to insulate the army from domestic political affairs.

Two acts of parliament gave the central government the legal powers to arrest members of the opposition. Even before the "Emergency" was declared the government passed the Maintenance of Internal Security Act (MISA) and the Defense of India Rules, both of which have been used on a large scale during the past year. Both acts precede the declaration of the "Emergency" and date back to the decision of the Indian government to call an "Emergency" in 1972 at the time of the war over Bangladesh. Technically speaking, India has been under an "Emergency" for several years. The difference is that the June 1975 declaration was based upon internal political disturbances while the previous emergency declarations were based upon external considerations. Under the MISA regulations the government could conduct arrests without habeas corpus, but after the "Emergency" was declared, an act of parliament has amended the MISA regulations so that the government may now arrest individuals without having to present a declaration of charges, even before a magistrate. What has disturbed many critics is not simply that those arrested do not have to hear their charges, but that no charges need be presented at all. Since the act has been amended, even if the "Emergency" is terminated, the government will continue to have the legal authority to arrest individuals without producing charges in a court of law.

The final institutional change that I'd like to briefly mention is the Youth Congress. Clearly, Mrs. Gandhi's decision to declare an "Emergency" was partly related to her own legal defeat in the high court, which called for her to vacate her parliamentary seat as a result of a violation of the election law, but it was also related to her concern over the declining electoral position of the Congress Party. Obviously she could no longer be sure that in the national parliamentary elections, due in early 1976, the Congress Party would emerge victorious. She had witnessed a major upheaval in the state of Bihar where a massive statewide campaign against the governing Congress Party led to the organizational collapse of Congress. There was a similar campaign in Gujarat after a Congress government resigned in the midst of a political crisis. In Gujarat an alliance of the opposition parties was widely heralded as a prototype for national opposition cooperation, and the elections in that state were widely seen as foreshadowing the elections of early 1976.

In a few states the Youth Congress offered itself as a new force to replace the decaying state party organization. The Youth Congress has existed for many years as the youth wing of the party, but in the late 1960s it emerged as an independent force in the state of West Bengal when a number of people in the Congress organization in Calcutta decided that the only way to break the power of the Communist Party-Marxist (CP-M) was to meet their violence with the violence of a more militant Congress. The Youth Congress recruited *goondas*, or "toughs," to play the same kind of game played by the violent Naxalites and the CP-M. The Youth Congress largely succeeded in breaking the back of the radical communist forces in Calcutta and the Congress party, led by Siddhartha Ray, a close associate of Mrs. Gandhi, swept the parliamentary elections in 1971 and the subsequent state assembly elections. The Youth Congress in Calcutta became something of a model for Youth Congress organizations in other cities. Mrs. Gandhi's son, Sanjay Gandhi, age 29, emerged as the key figure in building these cadre-based youth organizations. He was particularly active in the city of Delhi, and during the past year similar organizations have been created in the major cities throughout India. The Youth Congress has a lot of money and it attracts a rather different class of young people than have typically been attracted to political organizations. Perhaps because of Sanjay Gandhi's own involvement, people recognize that the Youth Congress is a critical vehicle for gaining political influence in the urban scene. Sanjay Gandhi also works closely with the former Chief Minister of the State of Haryana, Bansi Lal, India's new defense minister.

Incidentally, Bansi Lal recently achieved international publicity for a speech he made that captures the increasingly personalized atmosphere that has developed in Delhi. Addressing a large public meeting on his first return visit to his home district in Haryana after becoming a central minister, he said, "All my strength comes from the blessings of Shrimati Gandhi . . . whatever task she gives me I do with dedication." He then went on to explain that he was loyal to Indira Gandhi personally, not to the Office of the Prime Minister and that he would remain loyal to her all his life.

And so we move from Motilal to Jawaharlal, to Indira, to Sanjay, four generations of political leaders, each with quite different styles. Motilal and Jawaharlal were both constitutionalists, both committed to legal procedures, to individual rights, and to parliamentary institutions. Nehru, a figure of enormous popularity, could have followed Sukarno and Nkrumah in their quest for direct links with the masses without cumbersome intermediary institutions, but Nehru chose to work through these institutions. Mrs. Gandhi, in contrast, has clashed with her own party, sought to link herself directly with the masses, and endeavored to strengthen the institutions of coersion—the Research and Analysis Wing, and the central police units such as the Central Reserve Police, the Home Guards, the Border Security Force, and the Central Industrial Security Force.

Discussion

Pye:

There are perhaps three different ways in which this discussion can go. We could focus on the power relationships, we could focus more narrowly on the generational question, or we could ask about the role of authority in transforming so huge and diverse a society as India. Why has Mrs. Gandhi acted as she has? Where are we to look for an explanation?

Weiner:

One major difference between Mrs. Gandhi and her father was that her father was always secure in his power, while she was not. Jawaharlal Nehru always knew that his position as India's prime minister and as an international figure was as secure as could be. Indeed, from time to time in the 1950s Nehru threatened to resign when he clashed with the leadership of the Congress Party organization, but he knew full well that his resignation could never be accepted by the party leaders. But Mrs. Gandhi knew that when she was first chosen as prime minister following the death of Lal Bahadur Shastri, there were many senior party leaders who were opposed to her. She received support from two quarters, from a substantial number of state chief ministers and from Kamaraj Nadar, then President of the Congress Party. But support from within the party was far from overwhelming. After a period of inflation, following the decision to devalue the Indian rupee, and a narrow victory in the 1967 general elections, it became apparent that there were many Congress leaders who had second thoughts about her leadership. She then won the support of a left-of-center group within the Congress Party and began to pursue a set of populist measures in an effort to win popular support—for she clearly did not have the support of the party organization, the state chief ministers, and even many members of Parliament. It was this sense of her own political insecurity that led her to centralize authority, by strengthening her own Cabinet Secretariat, taking control of the Home Ministry, creating her own intelligence institutions, and strengthening and centralizing the police; and it also led her to turn against the institutions that threatened her position—first her own Congress Party, then the opposition, the press, and, finally, the courts.

Field:

There is a great deal of interest in the role that Sanjay is playing in the inner councils of Indian government at this point. To what extent is Sanjay an historical analogue to Rasputin? Indeed, what exactly is his role vis-à-vis his mother and vis-à-vis the Indian political system as a whole?

Weiner:

One of my central arguments is that as India has become more authoritarian and more centralized, many of the key institutions that played such an important role in the development of modern India have been eroding. Sanjay plays an important role in that the weakening of the party organization has tended to make the system fall back on personal relationships to a greater degree than ever before. Many Indians have commented on the almost dynastic quality of the system, and many assume that in time Sanjay will be selected as President of the Congress Party, following in the footsteps of his grandfather, father, and mother.

Mrs. Gandhi has turned to her son because there are so few other people she can trust. Moreover, she evidently sees him building a new popular organization—the Youth Congress—that can provide her with the element of popular support that she seeks, but cannot obtain through the regular Congress Party organization.

But there is some tension between mother and son, as Sanjay, in contrast with the leftist rhetoric of his mother, emphasizes right wing themes. Early in the "Emergency" he denounced the Communist Party of India, made statements critical of the Soviet Union, and spoke sympathetically of the plight of the business community encumbered by the regulations of the Indian bureaucracy. As India's political institutions—the opposition parties, the state Congress organizations, the press, and the courts—atrophy, we may very well see Sanjay seek to strengthen his relationship with the military through the defense minister, and by working closely with the business community and building up the Youth Congress to create a power base of his own.

One indication of his growing power in the last few months is that he has become a kind of troubleshooter for Mrs. Gandhi in dealing with some of the disputes within the state party organizations. It is also widely believed that in the Indian state of Uttar Pradesh, Sanjay was influential in choosing the new chief minister; similarly, Sanjay selected the leader of the Youth Congress. By choosing leaders he signaled to members of the Indian political elite that he is a man of considerable power, one whose power far exceeds any formal positions that he holds.

Dominguez:

My question concerns what is to follow. One possibility is that India is to become more simplified, more dependent upon individuals. However, you also mention a number of things that suggest the possibility that there is some resilience in India's democratic institutions. To the best of my knowledge, Mrs. Gandhi has made no claims to legitimate rule apart from the basic constitutional framework. She seemed to have "couped" within the accepted framework of politics; she has not yet obliterated institutional structures. There seems to remain a fair degree of pluralism in a country that has been characterized by its pluralism in the past. In your view, what lies ahead? Is it further simplification, further strengthening of an as-yet-incomplete authoritarianism, or is there to be an interplay between the two?

Weiner:

I must confess that I find it easier to describe what institutions Mrs. Gandhi has taken apart than those which she may propose to put in their place. She has spoken of major constitutional reforms. In early December a draft constitution was circulated among Congress leaders. That draft constitution called for the creation of a presidential system with a Supreme Council, to be headed by the president, which would have the authority to overrule the courts and to dismiss judges. This system was designed to circumvent the institution in India that stands in the way of wholly centralized power—the independent judiciary. Apparently that draft met with substantial opposition from within the Congress Party. Indeed, Mrs. Gandhi has gone so far as to repudiate that draft. It was obviously a trial balloon, and it does suggest, as you point out, that authoritarianism in India is not so well-entrenched that Mrs. Gandhi can do anything she would like.

But with that having been scrapped, it's left us more uncertain as to what the next step is to be. She has postponed the elections, and she has institutionalized many of the elements of the "Emergency," such as press censorship and arrests without trial. One wonders if even Mrs. Gandhi has any idea what India's political arrangements are to look like after the "Emergency" is over.

Griffith:

There are, in the case of India, a number of parallels with Germany in 1933, but there are even more parallels here with Mussolini's Italy. I would suggest that it would be useful to begin discussing the question of whether or not we are witnessing in India a peaceful transition to fascism. We have seen it in some Eastern European countries, and fascism seems to me to be a much-neglected phenomenon. I would also like to raise a question that is seldom raised in our JOSPOD discussions, that is, the question of American foreign policy. I think that I would disagree with Moynihan's views that we should be against India now because it is becoming fascist. After all, most of the world's nations are fascist. We just don't call them that. We call them other things. We should pay no more attention to the internal position of India on the question of democracy than we do in our relations with the Soviet Union. I think that we should be primarily concerned with India's attitude toward the United States. Now, it is in our interests to keep India hostile to the United States, if only because that hostility serves to maintain a friendship between the Soviet Union and India, which thus widens the Sino-Soviet dispute. We should encourage this situation by a policy toward India of "malign neglect."

Papanek:

I am struck by the frequency of press references to the fact that the British parliamentary institutions are no longer suitable for India. Do you see an expression in India today for what its new institutions will look like? Did you discern in your talks with Indians a concern about foreign intelligence communities in India? And third, is there concern in India with what any particular foreign individuals or nations think about the "Emergency"?

Weiner:

On the latter question, I think Mrs. Gandhi is particularly concerned with what outsiders think. This is demonstrated by the fact that she has been constantly critical of Western press treatment of the "Emergency." She has given frequent interviews to German, British, and Yugoslav journalists in order to make her case more strongly abroad. While she has frequently stated that the reaction in the West to the "Emergency" does not mean anything to her, it is clear from her statements that it does mean a great deal.

Let me answer your other questions by referring to the reaction of various other Indian groups to the "Emergency." The one group most hostile to the "Emergency" is, of course, the press. The newspapers are now trying desperately to maintain some degree of independence as a consequence not only of the censorship, but also of the government's efforts to gain direct control of the newspapers. There has been a running battle for the control of many of the major newspapers, for the control of the appointment of editors, and for the establishment of a central news agency.

The group most favorably disposed toward the "Emergency" is the bureaucracy. The bureaucracy has clearly gained the most. This is especially true of one particular bureaucratic group, the Prime Minister's Secretariat. This group was strengthened by Lal Bahadur Shastri to give the prime minister's office greater control over intelligence. Mrs. Gandhi has developed the secretariat into a forceful and powerful organization that now makes a large number of important policy decisions. Indeed, the Twenty Point Program itself did not come from the Congress Party or from the Parliament, but from the Prime Minister's Secretariat. It is a bureaucrats' program for national development.

Although the bureaucrats gained most from the "Emergency"—authoritarianism really meant a shift of power from parliamentary and party institutions to the bureaucracy—some of the older bureaucrats I met expressed their distress at the destruction of democratic institutions; they are most distressed by the erosion of the power of the judiciary, for the older bureaucrats have a great faith in legal institutions and in orderly procedures. The leading figures in the opposition arrested by Mrs. Gandhi—men like Jayaprakash Narayan and Moraji Desai—are of her father's generation. It does suggest that commitment to democratic institutions is a generational matter—that the generation of Jawaharlal Nehru believed in democratic institutions as something to be valued for their own sake, while the generation of Mrs. Gandhi and her close associates have a more instrumental view of politics. They justify what they have done partly by claiming that she saved the country from the disorder created by the democratic process, but more fundamentally by the economic changes that have since taken place and that they attribute to the "Emergency." What counts, her supporters argue, is how successful the government is in creating a strong, modern state and economy. The West is critical, she notes, not because India has ceased to be democratic, but because the West fears a strong India. In the past, many of India's leaders attributed their slow pace of change to the difficulties inherent in a democratic system requiring consensus. Mrs. Gandhi now justifies her efforts to rewrite the constitution and to create more centralized and authoritarian institutions by what she believes she will be able to accomplish. Legitimacy for Nehru was in the process; for Mrs. Gandhi it is in performance, especially in the economic realm. But since governments rarely perform in a way that meets the expectations of their followers, performance is always a precarious basis for political authority.

7

Generational Change in the Arab World

William Quandt

Ten years ago, when I first began to consider the topic of political generations in Algeria, I was concerned with the question of why there had been such an intense struggle within the political elite after independence.[a] In looking at the development of the nationalist movement, I found it useful to identify political generations, which I grouped into two general categories. There was first the initial liberal nationalist response to the French colonial presence. This was superceded by a more radical and younger generation of nationalists. I argued at that point that each of these generations seemed to emerge in reaction to what was perceived as a failure of the preceding one. The liberals tried to rely on legal-constitutional ways of gaining from the French increased autonomy, independence, and so forth. That effort failed dramatically in 1936. The next generation that came along used that failure as a point of reference. They saw what techniques did not work and thus they sought new ones such as mass political organizations and more forceful articulation of goals. They too failed in a rather dramatic fashion in the late 1940s. The French broke up their mass organization after World War II. The movement was driven underground. It spawned, in its turn, a third generation of more revolutionary nationalists who argued that both the liberals and their successors had failed conspicuously due to their reliance upon the established political framework. This generation was a bit younger and it broke starkly with the preceding generation as they argued for, and indeed employed, violence against the French rule.

We can also identify generations in Algeria whose introduction to politics came with the revolution itself. These young intellectuals and fighters had no roots in the preceding nationalist generations. These were the people who emerged after the assumption of independence as the dominant elite. The immediate postindependence period witnessed an intense struggle among these generations for control of the machinery of the state. While the revolutionaries initially succeeded, these groups tended to cancel each other out, and when the dust had settled by 1964–65, the new groups that seized power represented this third generation. They weren't people like Messali Hadj, Ferhat Abbas, or Ahmed Ben Bella. They were people who had entered politics during the revolution; they were ten to fifteen years younger than the Ben Bella generation; and once they gained control of the apparatus of the state, they've

---

[a]For this particular study, see the author's *Revolution and Political Leadership: Algeria 1954–1968* (Cambridge, Mass.: MIT Press, 1969).

been able to maintain stability. To date the faces have remained the same and things have been calm in Algeria.

All this suggests to me that concentrating on elite generations has value, particularly for predicting stability or change. It may also help us in predicting policy orientations. In particular, this Algerian elite has concentrated on internal development and security, and this is not at all surprising given their backgrounds in comparison to those who preceded them. Obviously, other factors such as class and ethnicity must also be considered in studying Middle East elites, and often these will explain more than generations. Generation is most useful in explaining major discontinuities over a long time period, not minor policy shifts from day to day.

The problem of expanding the focus from Algeria to the Arab world as a whole is that the Arab world is an immense and diverse place. To talk of it as a single entity is of course ridiculous, and to break it down into its major subsections is difficult. Nevertheless there are a few comparable features in this political cultural region. I'll try to deal with at least several cases within the Arab world, but first I should say a word about how I conceive of political generations.

First, I think that in the present state of affairs in the Arab world one has to concentrate on politics as an elite phenomenon. So too, in an analysis of political generations it is most useful to look at elites rather than to attempt to speak of a political generation that has some broad mass base. In most parts of the Arab world masses are still very much on the margin of national politics. The Palestinians may be one of the few exceptions, for they have been effectively politicized and traumatized because of the specific nature of their struggle.

In my thinking, a political generation is distinct from just a clique, a clan, or faction. It has to be something considerably broader than that. There is a size dimension to be considered, for a generation must be large enough to cut horizontally across other lines of cleavage. I would define a political generation in terms of shared political orientations toward the objectives of policy and the uses of power. On the whole this shared identity stems from two key sources: common experiences and/or a reaction to the previous generation. The combination of these helps to define a political generation, and this is clearly a subjective phenomenon. Having said that, I think it's clear that political generations can come more often than the every thirty years or so that we identify with biological generations. People are reacting to a wide variety of events, and the advent of a generation can be both rapid and awesome. There may be just a few years difference between one generation and another. I should also note that you will find on occasion the phenomenon of individuals moving from one generation to another. There is such a thing as intergenerational mobility that can come about through a sort of adult resocialization. Yet, this is certainly unusual.

In the Arab world power is normally held by a single generation. There are not many examples of diversity within the political elite; there are few cases of multigenerational participation. There are not many instances in which an elite has gradually absorbed new generations in an attempt to circulate the leaders; once power is captured by one of these political generations, there is a strong propensity to maintain the power without introducing new, and younger, elites to the rule. As a result, as challenges are suppressed, frustration builds among the younger generations, and when the break comes, it is a sharp one. The discontinuities can be very palpable between generations. So too, the policy discontinuities also will be quite marked. With the exception of the monarchies, political power in the Arab world tends to remain in one generation until there is a very sharp challenge. Very few old faces are then to be recognized in the circles of power.

In the Arab world as a whole, we can, on a very broad level, speak of two political generations that have either aspired to power or that have achieved power. The first of these is the generation of the nationalist movement. On the whole these nationalists were reacting against what preceded them. They were concerned more with gaining independence than with what they would accomplish after independence was achieved. They simply did not have a very rich socioeconomic content to their programs. These nationalists were the generation of Bourguiba and his associates in Tunisia; in Egypt, the generation of Sa'ad Zaghlul, the Wafd Party, and its successors; in Iraq, where the situation is a little more complex, the generation of Nuri as Sa'id, Rashid Ali, and a whole generation of politicians who worked within the mandate system to secure more and more autonomy from the British. In Morocco this group was the generation of the Istiqlal Party, Alal al-Fasi, and others, and it was perhaps a bit more traditional than the others I have mentioned. In the Algerian case this generation was that of Messali Hadj and Ferhat Abbas.

The interesting thing about this generation of politicians in the Arab world is that they had different results, different degrees of success. Bourguiba and his generation were very successful in Tunisia. They gained independence with a minimal amount of bloodshed, and the movement remained intact. The transition was carried off rather well, institutions were created, and a strong party apparatus emerged from the nationalist movement. Challenges to Bourguiba's power were harshly dealt with, and his position was quite firm. There was a great deal of turnover in the Cabinet, but the ministers were all of that generation and essentially were merely switching portfolios. The result has been that this government has become a rather staid oligarchy in Tunisia. There has been no new blood infused. The problem of succession thus looms very large, and the parallel to China here is very great. As a result, a whole generation of postindependence elites has been effectively barred from power, by being kept in minor bureaucratic posts and skipped over in a sense. The result may be that the transition may fall to an even younger, more radical group when the time comes.

Elsewhere this nationalist generation was much less successful. The Wafd Party in Egypt and, in a different sense, the Istiqlal Party in Morocco both failed to become the main arbiter of power in the postindependence period. The Wafd was alternately frustrated by the British and by the king. Indeed they were corrupted in the process. By the time the British hold over Egyptian politics was weakening, the Wafd had become a spent institution. The generation had been discredited and viewed as collaborationist. Instead, there was a proliferation of challengers such as Muslim Brethren, radical Marxist-Leninists, and younger army officers. When the change came, the Wafd did not survive the transition to the Nasser regime.

In the Moroccan case, the Istiqlal survived to independence, but by that time it too had spent its energies. The king had managed to capture the nationalist mystique because of his exile, and in the postindependence period he was very shrewdly able to minimize the role of the old nationalist elite. This generation was, in Morocco, one that grew old without really gaining political power. It was bypassed, by events, and it missed its opportunity to lead the postindependence state.

In the case of Algeria I think that it is also true that the early nationalists failed dramatically. One can make the case that Messali Hadj played as large a role in the nationalist movement as any individual; yet his name is anathema in Algeria today. He is never mentioned in the history books other than in passing and he has become a nonfigure. He completely missed his calling, and of course in the end he did collaborate with the French. Thus his efforts in the nationalist movement and his creation of the base of the FLN has been lost. Ferhat Abbas is likewise written off as an ineffectual and unimportant leader, although at one point he was without a doubt the most popular nationalist figure in Algeria.

In the Iraqi case we have a situation that is a bit comparable to the example of Tunisia in that the first generation of Iraqi nationalists, people like Nuri as Sa'id, did succeed to a large degree in gaining control of part of the institutions after semi-independence in 1932. From the 1920s until the 1950s this generation provided most of Iraq's leaders. Between 1921 and 1936 there were twenty-one cabinets that were formed from the same forty individuals. The same faces kept reappearing, and the remarkable thing is that these same faces were around into the 1940s and even the 1950s. Nuri himself was prime minister in 1958 when his entire generation was wiped out in one of the bloodiest coups d'etat of the Arab world. That is an example of the very sharp kind of discontinuity between one political generation and the next that I referred to earlier.

The second broad category of political generations in the Arab world can be called the postindependence generation for want of a better label. They break rather sharply with the first wave of nationalists. In general they seem to be more concerned with the content of independence, with the shape of things to come. They have the social, political, and economic programs that the previous generation did not possess. This generation was influenced by a number of events. In some parts of the Arab world the defeat in Palestine in 1947-48 was an important formative event that coincided with independence in Syria and Lebanon. In the countries surrounding Israel, the formation of political generations in reaction to the discrediting of those who held power and fought in Palestine can be sensed. In Arabic, in fact, there is a term for this generation. It is called the "generation of the disaster."

In the Egyptian case, the effect of the Palestine War and the resentment against the increasingly corrupt regime resulted in the emergence of a reformist movement within the army. The young officers launched the coup that toppled the monarchy in July 1952. Again, this was the kind of event that represented a sharp break, although it took about a year for the Nasser group to decide how thoroughly they wanted to break with the former elite. There was a transition period in which Farouk's son was named regent and in which some of the old guard politicians were kept in positions where they might play some role. But by 1953 it was clear that none of the old guard was going to survive the transition. So in Egypt a postmonarchical elite emerged that was very much reacting to the perceived failures of the previous generation of nationalists. I would argue that this is the generation that is still in control of Egypt today. Nasser of course held power for eighteen years, and Sadat is as close as anyone in Egyptian politics today can be to that generation. It was as a member of this generation that he learned his politics, and indeed it was he who announced the 1952 coup. If we look at the style of politics in Egypt today, we find somewhat more liberalization, but it is by and large the same political system. In foreign policy there has been a substantial change that involves Egypt's orientations toward the West and toward the USSR. That is a serious change, although we should recall that Nasser in his early days was viewed as a friend of the West. In terms of pan-Arabism there is also a difference, but it is partly due to the fact that Sadat cannot play the same role that Nasser did, for he has neither the resources nor the prestige to play that role. Indeed one could make the case that Nasser was drifting that way after 1967, and that Sadat has accelerated a trend that was visible in 1969-70. The point is that the faces are just not all that different today. While they might not be the Nasser intimates, they are by and large of the same generation. Sadat, while different as an individual from Nasser, is still a creature of the Nasser generation. There has not yet been a major transfusion of new blood.

I won't go through the other cases in detail, but we can point to the case of Iraq where there was a very sharp change in 1958. It involved a lot of sorting out of relationships among this suppressed generation that included Ba'athists, Communists, and Arab nationalists. It was entirely an intragenerational struggle among groups that had been frustrated by the previous elite. Typically when there is this sort of abrupt discontinuity, there is serious internal struggle within the ascendant generation. Once that is sorted out, there is likely to be a greater degree of stability. From 1968 to the present Iraq has had the same basic regime that has enjoyed an almost unparalleled stability.

There are some fundamental differences between the kinds of regimes I have been discussing and the monarchies with regard to the ways in which each deal with emerging political generations. Monarchs don't like competing political groups, and paradoxically we find in monarchies a greater propensity to coopt younger blood and to turn over personnel, as is true in Iran, in Jordan, and in Morocco. What we don't find is a whole generation being invited in by the king or challenging the king; the opposition is dealt with as individuals and people are coopted on that basis. The political generational phenomenon thus appears to be less significant in the monarchical systems.

Discussion

Abu-Odeh:

You have had quite a tall task set before you, for there are twenty-one members of the Arab League, and each has had its own experience. The Arab world is markedly diverse, and we cannot always identify only a preindependence and a postindependence generation. This is certainly true of some countries, and I would include in such a list Algeria, Morocco, Tunisia, and the Sudan.

I would say that there are three categories. The first is this preindependence to postindependence generational change. The second is the change from the monarchy to military rule as in Iraq. Finally there is the case of the monarchy that has not undergone any generational change due to its ability to infuse itself with new blood, as you've described.

There is another point to be made concerning your approach. In the Arab world there is no democracy. You put Arab rule in terms of the politics of the elite, but what I think is that to be more specific we should think in terms of tribal rule. Even in Lebanon, where there is an apparent democracy, there is a democracy based upon sects. In Morocco, the prime minister is the king's brother-in-law. In Algeria, Boumedienne's group is in fact a clan. In Tunisia the elite comes entirely from the coast; none come from the hinterland. In Egypt the speaker of the Parliament is the father of President Sadat's son-in-law. In Arabic this pattern is referred to as the "womb relationship." In Jordon, the general commander is the cousin of the king; the prime minister is his intimate friend from their school days. Saudi Arabia, Qatar, Bahrain, and Kuwait have even clearer cases of family rule. In Iraq most of those in power come from the village of Tikrit. So, whatever shape is given to rule in the Arab world, its basis is tribal.

Weiner:

Let me pursue that for a moment. We often think of a familial network as based upon hereditary traditions and frequently reinforced in contemporary scenes where the question of trust becomes central to political relationships. We also tend to think of generational politics where ideological concerns are paramount. Generational frameworks are usually employed where people, through a common experience, come to identify with one another's goals and vision of the world. If that were the case, then one would expect those countries in the Middle East where the problem of trust is acute to also rely upon familial networks. In those political systems where ideology is paramount, we would expect generational linkages to be somewhat more important. Is that the case?

Abu-Odeh:

I would caution Americans not to use their criteria to judge Arabs. The security affair is very acute in the Arab world, but I think the security issue is a cultural trait more than it is a matter of security. The relationships in the Arab world have usually involved "the boss." The boss had three main jobs: to protect the clan, to find new pastures, and to feed the clan. These three concerns have been transformed in modern times. The welfare state provides the food and the new pastures; protection is afforded the clan by the king or other leader through a loyal army. The same tasks have simply taken new forms.

So, I would discount the idea of generational change given this sort of framework.

Quandt:

I wouldn't want to challenge you on your own turf, on the topic of Arab culture. I think that the transition from Nasser to Sadat, for example, ought not to be addressed in generational terms. I don't think that the generational question is the most interesting one. I could argue perhaps that there is more continuity in terms of personnel, even though in the case of foreign policy there have been changes. Unlike Iraq in 1958, there was no sharp break in personnel; the faces are largely the same.

Your comments suggested that there is nothing new under the sun in the Arab world and that tribal politics remains the operational code. If that is the criteria, then Sadat hasn't changed anything at all. A patron-client sort of network still exists.

Sacks:

But the questions are rather different here. You might have the same patterns repeated even while there is generational change. Isn't the criterion that you are suggesting one of changes in personnel, or the influx of new faces?

Quandt:

Yes, that is how I conceive it. And in the case of Egypt that has not happened by and large. One of the implications of this example is that fairly substantial policy changes can occur without generational change.

Pye:

In the terms of our topic of generational politics, this implication raises a very important issue. If we cite very dramatic changes in policy and if we put them within the same generation, then we have a question of whether the generational framework is at all useful. We are clearly confronted with whether or not generations mean anything. Your study of Algeria was a strong case for the utility of this kind of analysis. But we've heard here of tribe and clan and other changes that cloud the concept of generations.

Quandt:

The question isn't one of whether generations explain everything or nothing. There is a limited range of political phenomena that can be usefully viewed from a generational perspective in the Middle East. In some systems, it is more useful than in others. Its utility depends on the questions we want to answer.

Huntington:

I'd like to add to that. We've spoken a great deal of the shifts from the colonial to the independence generation. But it seems to me that the point has been raised here in a variety of ways as to whether or not we are really discussing generations in the Arab world. One thing that members of a generation have to have in common is their date of birth. In a real sense this factor serves to distinguish one generation from another. A generation becomes politically significant when those born at approximately the same time experience some common event that shapes their orientations. This experience gives political meaning and coherence to a generational cohort.

Now, as you were taking us through a series of cases in the Arab world I couldn't help but wonder if what you were describing was at all generational. Were these merely cases of cliques, groups, classes, clans, or factions seeking power? The example of the tribe that has been suggested here is absolutely counter to the idea of a generation. A clan is a structure that runs vertical in time, not horizontal. This sort of connection cuts across generations, whereas generations are horizontal networks that ideally cut across these other sorts of cleavages.

Another way to look at this issue is to suggest the possibility of a major change in personnel that is not a generational change. When Nasser came to power there was a generational change, but there were other changes as well. There was a military taking over, there may have been a class change, and so forth. There may be other more fruitful ways to look at these transitions. The same things might have been true in Iraq in 1958. There may have been several cleavages equally or more significant than the generational one.

So, there are two questions here. We need to examine whether regional or ethnic or generational or class or some other cleavage is most important in explaining change. Secondly, we have to differentiate between a change in personnel and a generational change.

Quandt:

In the case of Libya there was an age-specific change. There was a twenty- to thirty-year age difference in the shift from the monarchy to the next regime. These were people with significantly different attitudes and programs that were Nasserist influenced. They were, on the whole, Arab nationalist in foreign policy orientation and Islamic socialist in domestic policy. On both counts, they differed substantially from the old elite. In practical politics, the new leaders acted differently also. They moved against the oil industry in stages, beginning in 1971; they pressed for unity with Egypt. In order to grasp the differences between the old and new regimes, a generational perspective is necessary.

Abu-Odeh:

In the case of Syria this sort of generational shift happened once. It happened with the change to the military. Here the idea of generational change from the preindependence generation is applicable.

Quandt:

Yes, those are the cases where I can see that the changes were linked in a real sense to generational divisions. But, I'm not sure that if I wanted to understand the politics of Iraq today, for example, that I'd ask generational questions. If I wanted to compare Iraq today to Iraq fifty or eighty years ago, perhaps I would. But to examine Iraq today I would ask Adnan's question, that is, who is related to whom? Where do they come from? What is their power base and so forth? Certainly family ties are one of the strongest bonds in the Arab world. It is clear that the concept of generations has little utility in monarchical systems where the patron-client ties are strong and where the cooptation strategy is pursued.

Bennett:

One of the things that we have not adequately discussed are those salient events that shape generations. Perhaps one of the problems in attempting to identify discrete generations in the Middle East is the fact that nothing terribly galvanizing has happened in the last twenty-five years. But that leads to another point that has not yet been touched upon. In the last three years enormous kinds of changes that might be potentially salient in the formation of generations have taken place. What impact in this regard can you see from the new oil wealth for example?

Quandt:

The 1973 OAPEC successes had the effect of allowing the Arab nations to feel better about themselves. In a way it served to offset the disappointments and self-recriminations that came with the 1967 Arab-Israeli War. There are in fact two generations to speak of here. The first is that of the Palestinian *fedayeen* who split from the PLO after 1967, and the other is the equally young Arab generation that has become connected with the oil enterprises. We can speak of "Petro ethics" and the attitudes of young Arabs. So there is a real tension between the militance of some and the attachment to wealth of others.

Abu-Odeh:

I would agree that there are two generations in the wings. One is attached to the outcome of the Arab-Israeli conflict. These people are left with only one alternative. Since 1950 the Arabs always had three or four alternatives in dealing with this question. When they were defeated in 1948, the people blamed the reactionary rulers. When Nasser came, the people thought that this charismatic leader would succeed, but when, in 1967, he failed, so too did the alternative of the progressive military ruler. Then there is the third alternative, that of the popular liberation war. Here too the people believe they have failed.

Now there are those who believe that the Arabs have been left with only one alternative that has not been yet attempted: the restructuring of the Arab world. I would say that one of the generations that we might expect to emerge is comprised of these intellectuals and university graduates.

There is also another generation, but it is less activist, for it lacks a social vision. This generation has been educated via the television. It is oriented toward the West through the media. The members are aware of the wealth that they are going to inherit. This generation will be the next one if the Arab-Israeli conflict is solved. If it is not, the stage will be given to the first group—those who believe in the restructuring of the Arab world.

Huntington:

Let me shift the focus for a moment from the national level to the subnational. I'd like to take a look at generational change within particular institutions. One of the things that has always struck me in looking at political parties in Latin America is that there is a very strong tendency for parties to extend themselves beyond the founders' generation. Often the party will wither as a result. You did mention some of the parties of the Arab world. How do you view the process of generational change within them?

Quandt:

Of course, political parties have not been very strong in the Arab world with perhaps only a couple of exceptions. The Istiqlal has withered. It did not make the transition because it split along generational lines, Istiqlal-UNFP. Neither was Wafd able to appeal across generational lines. The Ba'ath has kept the name, but one could argue that the factions within it are split along generational lines. With the exception of the Ba'ath in Iraq the parties in the Middle East have very much fallen prey to the kind of process that you've described.

Weiner:

In your description of generational cohorts you focused on commonly shared political outlooks and preferences. We can also look at how the educated sector of a generation changes over time in relation to their occupational preferences. One of the simplest distinctions may be that the most able and best educated chose the bureaucracy at the time of independence, whereas now they might choose the oil-related industries. Do there seem to be generational patterns of occupational preferences?

Quadt:

In those societies where the private sector is booming, I believe that it has had a serious impact upon career choice. The bureaucracy can no longer compete with the private sector. In a country like Iraq, where the oil sector is large but where it is state controlled, positions in the government are still sought after. In other states the lure of the Gulf is strong. Emigration is chosen by the ablest.

Weiner:

What you are suggesting then is that there may be intragenerational conflicts taking shape between those pursuing wealth through petro-employment and those seeking power through government positions.

Quadt:

Indeed, and in fact these occupational choices may reflect class cleavages as well. We may find lower-class persons stepping up into the same bureaucracy that does not appeal to the most educated.

8

Generational Change in the Israeli Political Elite

Amos Perlmutter

What would have taken a more leisurely natural course was accelerated by the flow of events in Israel after the 1973 war. The Israeli political system, dominated by the House of Labor (the labor movement and its satellites in the government, agriculture, and industry), has been challenged by its society. What are the major signposts of change in the Israeli political system since 1973? First, we witnessed the decline of the *Parteistat*, the party-dominated state. Second, there was the decline of the political voluntarism so prominent in the pre-1948 Yisuv (Jewish community in Palestine). Third, there was a thaw in the rule of the gerontocracy in the House of Labor and the decline of the pioneer seniority system. Fourth, there was the end of the exclusive rule of the apparatchiks, and with this the system of personalism, protectionism, and restrictive political recruitment came to a halt. A new military-bureaucratic elite was beginning to replace the apparatchiks of what I call the former *voluntary* Bolshevik system. There was also a concomitant decline of authority and the rise of governmental activity. We can point to the use, but not yet the consolidation of, extra-political centers comprised of (1) the military, (2) the skilled technocrats, and (3) the intellectuals.

If this is the background in Israel from 1967 to the present, exacerbated by the events of 1973, what about generational continuity in Israel's operative leadership-authority system? I am going to argue that there is a generational continuity, but that there has been a change of style, performance, and behavior among the Israeli political elite. We can divide Israel into two clusters of political generations. One I will call the Bolshevik generation, and the other the state generation. Thus, I could have entitled this chapter "The Founding Fathers and their Spoiled Children of the State."

The first generation's qualities can be explained in terms of political culture, composition, performance, skill, type of rule, and dynamics. It is not difficult at all to speak of the founding fathers as a generation that ruled Israel without any opposition between 1920 and 1960. The opposition that existed can also be seen as founders of the state even though they did not participate in ruling. They did not participate in the rule because they were prevented by the Bolsheviks of the House of Labor from doing so until 1949–50 when the State of Israel was established. So, among these founding fathers, or revolutionary political activists, there are two groups: ideologists and apparatchiks. The ideologues were few. They set the institutional and conceptual framework for the Jewish socialist state. But it was the apparatchiks in the trade-union movement, in cooperative movements, and in the Labor Party itself that really maintained and sustained the organization, the party, and eventually the state.

The career of David Ben-Gurion is the most illustrating example of how one member of the ideological group emerges over the others, not because of charisma but because of the apparats. In 1925 he was recruiting party members and was organizing professional party members, that is, the people who speak about socialist Zionism, and who spoke about farming the kibbutz, but who never farmed the kibbutz. They were recruited from the Russian, Galician, and Polish socialist Zionist movements. These apparats came directly to the offices of the party and of the Histadrut and acted as Ben-Gurion's party machinery. They account for his very emergence to power. His rise to power was not unlike Lenin's—a man whom Ben-Gurion both studied and admired. Under the facade of ideology a powerful social democratic, yet restrictive, political system was established. The passage of entry was given only on the basis of ideological belongedness, on participation in the movement, and on the basis of contributions to the state as defined by Ben-Gurion and his apparats.

In no time at all, Ben-Gurion was able to totally dominate the party. Using the party as an organization, he was able to take over the Jewish community in Palestine, the Yishuv. Later, he was to use that same instrument to dominate the World Zionist Organization and all of Jewish financial support for Israel. This is the sense of voluntary but nevertheless political Bolshevism that I have been trying to convey. Ben-Gurion was a man who understood well the relationship between ideology and organization. He understood that the building of a state requires the building of an apparat. This apparat was made up of people who possessed skills that were essential to the task before them: They were trade-unionists, mobilizers of men and resources, agitators, and propagandists. They had never been interested in elections until 1949. Between 1905 and 1949 there were only four elections of the General Assembly of the Jewish community in Palestine. Even then, only twenty percent to thirty percent of the people voted, and the Labor Party organized its support for victory quite easily. In the building of the state, the party was not very concerned with electoral behavior. Indeed, there was contempt for electoral behavior in the sense that it would involve coming down to the people to campaign, to shake hands.

The opposite happened after 1967. But perhaps first I should point out what did happen, so that we've a means to understand the generational context of the Israeli elite. The organization succeeded beyond its own imagination in every aspect possible. It succeeded in kibbutz building, in organizing the workers, in dominating Jewish money at home and abroad, and in ostracizing the opposition. Restricted as the elite was, it could build up only the most meager of successor groups. It was usually comprised of younger apparatchiks of the youth movements. For instance, Shimon Peres, Minister of Defense, was actually an apparatchik of the Noar Oved, the Working Youth, which was a youth movement organization. Two or three others who are in the Israeli cabinet—the minister of housing, for example—are also former apparatchiks of the youth movement. Here and there a few sons of the apparatchiks, who were apparatchiks of the youth movements themselves, have moved in. No other modern men of Israel, with the exception of the military, to our own day could enter the political leadership of the state. Even among the military, these people were the sons of apparatchiks. Take the example of Yitzhak Rabin. His mother, Rosa Cohen, was a very famous leader of the women's organization of the party. Some have argued that Israel is being taken over by the military, but they are wrong. It has been taken over by the sons of the apparatchiks, among whom were successful military men. A famous one is of course Moshe Dayan. I can name them one after another, Chaim Bar-Lev, the four in the present Israeli Cabinet, Israeli generals, and the rest. There is little concern among the Rabins, and the military sons of the apparatichik-ideologues for the need to do party work. They are like spoiled children in a way, and Golda Meir would be the first one to point that out.

To conclude, I would just point out that there is continuity, but performance is different. So too the confidence of the electorate is different. Meir, Ben-Gurion, and even Eshkol were virtually the law. Rabin cannot achieve that type of legitimacy and acceptance in Israel. There is a Cabinet now (1976-77) that is dominated by three ministers. The prime minister was formerly a deputy to Foreign Minister Allon. In 1948, in the Palmach, Allon was the commander of the Palmach, assisted by Rabin. I don't see how it is possible for Allon to accept that his deputy in the revolutionary movement is now his boss. Shimon Peres, the third minister, worked very hard for close to thirty-five years as a young apparat. He doesn't have a great deal of respect for Rabin. So, there are three individuals who are running the government who don't have respect for each other in spite of the fact that each one of them has a tremendous record.

I don't see any change in terms of generation. I don't see Rabin as a man who has the ability to regroup the old Bolshevik party. Therefore, to his convenience, he is in coalition with the younger apparatchiks of the trade union organization, of the party, and of both urban and rural organizations. He is not an ideologue, he is without experience in party organization. Yet the party needs him more than he needs them because the party is afraid of a takeover either by the left (Allon) or by the right (Peres and Dayan).

The decline from voluntary Bolshevism to managerial, military individuals demonstrates different performance. The style and performance are different. I don't see any revolutionary change, for the continuity is there. There is no individual either within the party or outside the party with greater imagination than those who rule the country.

There is of course a point to be made concerning the Arab-Isreali conflict. People always ask me about the impact of the conflict upon Israeli politics. I must answer that there is very little impact when it comes to the sort of thing that I have addressed in this chapter. Domestic politics and the structure of internal politics are not influenced by the conflict. The politicians neither survive nor die by it. They may be catalyzed by it as they were in 1967. Abdul Nasser imposed upon the party the reign of Dayan. Sadat has hastened the process of the collapse of the gerontocracy of the old Bolsheviks. But it could just as well have happened in 1969.

Discussion

Isaacs:

Could you say a word about the under-thirty-five generation in Israel? You've not mentioned who it is that is coming up behind these leaders. To what extent are the under-thirty-fives significant in the political process?

Perlmutter:

Forty years of party rule has created a deep contempt for the party apparatus. The young Israeli feels it beneath his dignity to be a party apparatchik. But many young Israelis would like to be leaders of the state by virtue of their modern skills, be they engineers, doctors, architects, or lawyers. But they are unwilling to understand that in order to succeed, they have to do some party work. And this is looked upon contemptuously by the modern young men. They are actually cutting their own branch.

Huntington:

I've two questions. First, to follow up on your last comments, perhaps these young Israelis are correct about the role of the party. It may be that they correctly perceive the party as fading, while they, the technocrats, are rising on the horizon. Secondly, I have trouble reconciling your characterization of the "spoiled children" generation. Which are they, petulant sons who weren't terribly serious, or managers? Did they merely inherit their positions as sons of the elite or do they bring themselves to power by virtue of their managerial talent?

Perlmutter:

On the latter point, the answer is that it is a combination of the two. It is not sufficient to be a manager or a military man; one also has to be the son of a founding father. This point is most vivid in the case of Rabin, as the son of Rosa Cohen.

As to your first question, we must wonder how these young technocrats are to come to power. If the apparatchiks in the 1950s, in coalition with the military, are very powerful, why would they allow these young technocrats to enter politics? They will give them positions in the bureacracy and in the foreign service, but they will not give them positions of importance in the Cabinet or the Histradut. The party has not died, it is in the process of decay.

Pye:

Your characterization of the founders of the Israeli state as "voluntary Bolsheviks" strikes me as extraordinary for it has enormous implications for a comparison to China. Here are two societies in which the elite has stressed a return to the countryside. In both societies meritocracy is their best payoff. Yet, they both are committed to pretending that this is not important. What you are saying about the Israeli situation indicates that the Israelis are about a half step ahead of the Chinese.

Perlmutter:

I've also recognized the great similarities here. I've written on a comparison of the processes of institutionalization in Israel and China. I've also compared the Chinese and Israeli militaries. There are tremendous similarities in the concept of the revolutionary soldier. The revolutionary soldier, as distinguished from the classical and the praetorian soldier, is dedicated to the defense of professionalism as the independent and exclusive property of the military. He is non- or anti-corporate and is on the whole noninterventionist. Yet, in both Israel and China, the revolutionary soldier rejected the traditional boundaries of civil-military relations, although never at the expense of civilian authority. In fact, what distinguishes both China and Israel is the supremacy of civilian authority in states under permanent garrison conditions.

Bell:

What I find missing in a sense in your account is the role of the hero and the role of virtue, the active component of ideology. I don't doubt in the least your description of Ben-Gurion as a man who emerged by the apparatchik. I can find, I am sure, many similar stories of popes or trade union leaders in New York. What is missing, however, is the nature of the commitment that binds their efforts. This is the important story. As someone once said about David Dubinsky, his nostalgia for socialism is like the nostalgia of a Wall Street banker for his Iowa childhood. As you get older this becomes more important to you. It is the changing nature of these people's commitments that, in the end, is the important aspect of what they are all about.

Perlmutter:

I have argued a revisionist line of my own here. I, too, used to speak of the symbiotic relationships between ideology and organization. There is no question but that here we are dealing with people possessing a great commitment. But my task in this discussion was a bit different. If I would begin with the Zionist proclamation, I would start by pointing out that if there is any one nation among the developing nations that has really succeeded in combining ideals and reality, it is Israel.

But there were fifty people with Ben-Gurion's commitment, yet there was only one Ben-Gurion, who emerged above the rest because of the apparat—not because he had more or less commitment than the others. I have had to ask why *he* emerged as first among the equals. It was he who understood that it was the organization of the apparat that would make him preeminent.

Haviland:

You have suggested that the Arab-Israeli conflict has not had a very significant impact upon domestic politics in Israel. I would think that it must have had a tremendous impact, especially as regards consensus building. The conflict can be regarded as what is providing as much consensus as there is in Israeli society. I would suggest that once this is solved that there would be much greater conflict in Israeli politics. The question is: In what directions will these splits evolve? On what issues and with the participation of what groups will Israel be divided?

Perlmutter:

I would say first that there is no palpable difference between the pioneer generation and the present generation concerning this commitment to peace. Yet there are no new solutions being offered either. Rabin and each member of his cabinet perceive the Arab-Israeli conflict no differently than any other cabinet of the last twenty years. I cannot feel confident at all in speaking of a postconflict Israel. When you speak to Israelis about such a postconflict period, they begin to feel like Christian Lebanese.

Huntington:

It seems to me that one of the characteristics of different generations is the cleavages that divide them. I wonder if you could elaborate a bit upon the ways in which the cleavages in the current generation differ from those of earlier generations. What are the consequences of these cleavages for the future evolution of Israeli society? In particular, I am concerned with the relationship between these cleavages and Israeli foreign policy.

Perlmutter:

The most serious cleavage is, of course, religion. Religion and civil rights are closely connected. First, there is the question of whether or not there can be secular marriage. That cleavage doesn't reflect the differences within the Labor Party, but it is reflected among the opposition parties. The question of what is a Jew is no longer a philosophical one. It is a political question par excellence, and it is a very serious cleavage for this generation. Although I would say that the cleavage was there in the older generation, it has never been as serious as it is now.

Secondly, there is the role of the non-European Jew, who doesn't get a break in any of the political parties. The Likud Party receives per capita, among the important parties of Israel, most votes from the Oriental Jews, but the party is no more representative of Oriental Jews than the Labor Party. This is also true of the Arab minority. It is a very important cleavage both for foreign as well as domestic policy.

The cleavages that I have mentioned all constitute challenges to original Zionism. Original Zionism was an attempt to establish a secular Jewish state, and it did not even perceive these difference among Jews from different parts of the Diaspora. Nor did it perceive the Arab question at all.

Finally, a most serious issue is that of foreign policy. I have trouble speaking of this in terms of a cleavage. I think Henry Kissinger would have to agree with me that the differences among Allon, Rabin, and Peres on foreign policy, to use his language, are not significant. I would say that the differences between the hawks and the doves in the Cabinet, with the exception of the question of the western bank, is not substantial. Before the Lebanese affair, it was perhaps slightly more an issue than it is now. The Israeli media has broadcast the Jordanian and Lebanese accounts of the fighting, and you can't imagine how watching the conflict in Lebanon changed the whole attitude toward Palestine. There are no doves who speak on Palestine now.

All in all, I see a consensual society with the absence of any cleavages serious enough to tear it apart. I reiterate my major thesis that the basic political fact in Israel today is generational continuity. The differences are in style, procedure, and behavior. The prior generation was composed of ideologues and apparatchiks—*Weltanschauungen* people. The latter generation is one of pragmatic, bureaucratic, and technocratic leaders. The generational conflict and cleavages in Israel would not be very significant except that the technocrats would be in no position to reestablish or revive the same style of political party movement type if the need arose. The cleavages among generations will evolve toward meritocracy, as versus the mere demonstration of zeal for the cause.

Pool:

What is the future of the religious parties in Israel?

Perlmutter:

I have had close contract with the National Religious Party, and I have found that the only dedicated Zionist, nationalist, cohesive, powerful organization is the National Religious Party. It has money from the Mizrachi organization, which is very powerful in the United States (it is estimated to have some two million members). The members are young and modern men, not unlike the Jesuits in the Catholic Church. The younger generation of the religious party are very different from the older generation in ideology and structure. They differ in terms of their attitude toward the state. The older generation was more militant concerning the secular state. They had defined religion and politics as identical. The younger generation found a hyphen between the two. Secondly, they had gone headlong into the pioneer effort. The younger generation has been most active in the new kibbutzim, the new settlements. Also, they have abandoned the middle-class, conservative, bourgeois spirit of the older generation in the National Religious Party. They, in fact, may be the key to the maintenance of the Rabin government. We will have to see what happens in the next election.

Migdal:

I have several comments on what you've already noted that I'd like to mention, before I get to my question. I'll agree that the ideals of Zionism are embedded in the Gush Emunim; we can see the zeal and the vision there. They are the only group that is expressing such a vision. Their ability to mobilize is based on this. There is a good deal of opposition to them, but it is a grumbling opposition. There is no one presenting an alternative vision, and this is where the anger toward Rabin is coming from. People are demanding an alternative vision from him; they claim that he is being immobilized and thus is having his own position undercut. They are providing an ideology that Rabin et al. do not have.

But I also disagree with you in that this Gush Emunim is not tied to the National Religious Party in any formal way. In fact, the National Religious Party has lost control of the Gush Emunim. How Gush Emunim will vote is very much in question. Many of them may go for the Likud, which has been pandering to them. I think that it is a mistake to look for structural or ideological connections between the National Religious Party and even its young wing and the Gush Emunim.

My question concerns your conception of the apparats. On the one hand, you said that the way Ben-Gurion institutionalized the system was to have apparats build the party and mobilize the public. This was your Bolshevik analogy. A bit later you noted that engineers, intellectuals, and others could never get involved in a political process that was monopolized by these apparats. Of course intellectuals, lawyers, and these people couldn't get involved in politics, because as soon as they did, they would become apparats and would no longer be identified by their previous occupational roles. This characterization bothered me especially when you talked about the current situation, because you said that the problem with the young generation was that they didn't care to do party work. You were accusing them of not being apparats.

Perlmutter:

The Bolshevik generation represented and integrated every aspect of society. All sorts of professionals were involved. Now, I should have defined what I meant by apparat. These are the permanent professional revolutionaries who work for the party day in and day out.

I was talking about the second-generation lack of leadership and vision required to integrate all these people as the pioneer generation had.

Bell:

But the questions of what is an apparat when there is a movement prior to the formation of a state and of what is an apparat after the creation of a state are different ones.

Perlmutter:

Well, perhaps I should make clear the differences between professional revolutionaries, party activists, and so forth. Israel does not have the sort of thing that exists in the United States. The American type of volunteer who goes out canvassing for a presidential candidate is not found in Israel. The only group that will do political work are those who are institutionalized and bureaucratized in the apparat system or in the House of Labor complex. You don't have the same type of political activism. It is a society in which more people vote than in most democracies. The people are opinionated on issues, but when it comes to other forms of political participation, there is very meager activity. I have not called for the return of the apparat, but there is a real apathy when it comes to political activity—the government as well as the opposition have closed political systems.

Dominquez:

I'm going to purposely distort your remarks, and I expect that you are going to disagree with what I have to say. At the elite level, after the establishment of the state, the issue of vision as a possible organizing feature has been a fraud for thirty years. It was a fraud before 1975, and it is a fraud now. The kind of fraud is different, but it is a fraud. There is no vision. It is the politics of personalism, position, and the politics of grabbing at straws or organizations.

At the mass level, there were a number of features that were fixed in time, but the cleavages do not vary from generation to generation, except perhaps in the National Religious Party. Israeli society as a whole has lost its dynamic, its history; it has no chance of renovation. It reached a point in time, in the 1940s, and it stopped. In terms of the theme of generational politics, it seems that your remarks can be distorted to point out that you are describing a society that is generationally static. As you have described it, Israeli society has no vision, no cleavages, no possibility for mobilization; it has personalized apparat.

So, I would like to hear you disagree with all of the points that I have raised: (1) that it is a fraud at the elite level, that the only thing that has changed is the kind of fraud; (2) that it is a society that has no cleavages and divisions that would lead to a sense of internal dynamic; and (3) that it doesn't have a generational dynamic in the sense of progress. If you can respond to this, then perhaps my initial puzzlement can be dispelled.

Perlmutter:

Yes, that is not what I mean. In the terms in which you've rephrased my comments, none is true. To begin with, I have never said that the true Bolsheviks are frauds. I think that it was Daniel Bell who pointed out earlier in our discussion that there are no true Bolsheviks at all in the Soviet Union. I would have to use Isaac Deutscher's phrase "The Armed Prophet" to describe David Ben-Gurion. Ben-Gurion understood that in order to establish a humanitarian Jewish state, he would have to take the Diaspora nation and move the people through the forty hard years of desert life. If you look upon the religion of labor and the conquest of the land theory, there is no question that there was no fraud whatsoever. Ben-Gurion also understood that it is not possible to maintain this momentum without an apparat, without financial support, without a flood of new recruits.

First and foremost, Ben-Gurion said that the Israelis need a government of laws. He was a stickler for laws, for rules, for an established system that is not based upon word of mouth. He was a devotee of the concept of *mamlachtiyut*, which literally means kingdom, but which can more accurately be translated as the need of the Jewish nation to have an organization to preserve its survival. In other words, what is the concept of Zionism? The Jews had no state and therefore could not survive as a full people. The argument among Zionists today is that a Jew is probably more secure in Boston today than he is in the Golan Heights. But he undoubtedly has a different identity. I should just say that things are not as they used to be, but neither is Israel a nineteenth-century Latin American state.

By generational dynamics, I certainly do not speak of a revolutionary change. I suppose real revolutions are rare and the Zionist revolution had taken place almost a century ago. The absence of a so-called generational dynamic doesn't mean that it was stultified and decayed in Israel. It only means that the sons of the Zionist pioneers are continuing the labor of their parents in procedurally and stylistically different ways. Generational continuity is a political concept that also describes a type of political behavior. In the case of the Rabin-Peres-Sharon generation, it means the preservation of the state's security and the ushering of Israel into the next century.

China: The Politics of Gerontocracy

Lucian W. Pye

I would like to divide the topic of my presentation into three parts. First, I plan to talk about the question of generations with respect to China and succession to Chairman Mao in particular. Second, I would like to address more generally the topic of gerontocracy, the practice of old men wielding power. Third, what runs through all of this, but deserves special attention, is the problem of the passing on of revolutionary fervor from one generation to the next. In the case of China, it is especially relevant to ask how leaders might demobilize a highly mobilized society, once the immediate rationale for mobilization has passed. In some ways, I think that the problem of succession of generations in China strikes at the heart of this last problem.

We can be quite brief on the first of these topics—the problem of the succession to Mao—because the subject has been discussed for more than ten years. Doak Barnett's (1967) *China After Mao* was written in a style that suggested that it was dealing with matters near at hand. This was a rather bold act on the part of Barnett because at the time many observers were convinced that the Chinese leaders, Mao Tse-tung and Chiang Kai-shek had achieved immortality out of the depths of their enmity toward each other: Neither would die until the other one did. Last year, though, Chiang died and of course now we have ominous reports on Mao's health. Maybe Chiang gave up the fight not because he was older, but because he had solved his succession problem and he knew that Mao hadn't solved his. Incidentally, few people seem to appreciate Chiang's ingenious use of the most traditional method of passing on power—he gave it to his son. Thus, an amazing phenomenon occurred on Taiwan: A republic, with all the symbols of republicanism, reverted to the imperial system of father-to-son power transference. This reversion to the oldest and easiest form of succession was hardly noticed abroad as most observers focused only on the matter of stability and continuing economic growth.

What I am going to talk about here are some of the reasons why the generational transference of power has been more difficult on the Mainland. The problem of succession to Mao is an old story in part because the issue emerged quite some time ago. In some ways the Cultural Revolution was a prelude, indeed it may have been the culmination, of that issue. One cannot really understand what happened in both the ideological and the power struggles that took place between 1966 and 1969 without considering the succession question. What stands out in this regard, and indeed what concerns us here, is the degree to which the Chinese succession problem can best be understood as a struggle among generations.

107

In China, the political generations are extraordinarily sharply defined. China is a society that has produced, oddly as a result of revolution, a highly refined layering of generations. This is peculiar because we think of revolutions as producing chaos, confusion, and disorder; yet there is a remarkably ordered structuring of political generations in China. Let me very briefly identify these. The first, and still the grand generation, is the one that participated in the Long March, the generation of Chairman Mao and of nearly all of the people who have been and still are in the ruling circles. This generation has been extraordinarily slow in giving up power. It is now an aging generation, but we should remember that the average age of those who made the Long March was only about nineteen, and therefore it is not entirely surprising that they have been around so long. All of the erstwhile designated successors to Mao—Liu Shao-ch'i, Lin Piao, Teng Hsiao-p'ing—were part of this generation. It is embarrassing for China specialists to have to admit that they don't know very much about the background of the current heir apparent, Hua Kuo-feng, but he does appear to be of an age to have possibly have been a part of this generation, or if not, certainly he was of the next. The second generation joined the Communist Party during the Yenan period and the Japanese War period; in some respects this is a split generation in the sense that elements of it came to the party out in Shensi while others joined the movement in the various base areas behind the Japanese lines. Sociologically, this generation was composed of a mixture of educated urban men and women who had fled from the cities of East China and rural interior people who joined the party because it happened to be where they were.

The third generation is the one that joined the Communist Party during the civil war against the Kuomintang. This generation was predominantly rural and came to communism through the channel of military service. The next generation entered the party in 1949 at the time of "Liberation." This is a very large generation since the party at that time mushroomed after victory. It is a generation that has always been seen by some of the older cadres as being composed of possible opportunists. Then there is the Korean War generation composed of those who were doubtful as to where China was going, but who, at the time of the Korean War, yielded to pressure and to the spirit of nationalism and joined the party. Finally, of course, there is now the generation that is coming to the party through the normal processes of youth recruitment and service in the Pioneers and the Young Communist League.

The very vividness of each of these generations provides testimony for the fact that the Chinese revolution was a highly managed and well-organized one. Those who came into the party at one period tended to move ahead in almost lockstep fashion and in time they became a ceiling above those who followed them at the next phase when the party significantly expanded. The generations tended to cling together not only because of their common socialization experience but also because the Chinese concept of "comradely behavior" includes the notion of not passing over those who have been in the cue line for power for some time. In nearly every organization, institution, and industry, we find that those who were there first have tended to hold on to power and to rank those who have come later according to the principles of seniority. This pattern explains what might seem to be the paradox that a revolutionary society should end up with very vivid generations and in time transform itself into a gerontocracy.

Another oddity is that the sharply layered generations have also produced the only pronounced cross-cutting basis for competitive political organization, the functional or "system" groupings. The recruitment pattern in China has been for the cadres to join some particular functional system—such as agriculture, industry, foreign affairs, the military, and so forth—and to have their entire careers within the function. To an amazing degree even managers in industry tend to stick with the same product line such as textiles, steel, heavy machinery, light industry, and so forth. Once the new recruit has been assigned to some activity, his entire career has been largely defined for him. The lack of flexibility in movement from one functional activity to another contributes to the generational pressures in that promotion is limited almost entirely to the process of retirement or purging. There are very few lateral transfers and thus everybody tends to become cued up in his particular functional activity.

All of this would be quite simple if we were to settle for being Floyd Hunter (1953), looking at our "Atlanta" from afar. We did see very clearly a power structure and a power elite. But in fact we are political scientists and interested in the interplay of politics. Therefore, if we look at China more in the spirit of how Robert Dahl (1962) viewed New Haven, we are quick to see that Chinese politics consists of the interplaying of generations and cross-cutting functional interests. In some respects it is easier to identify the generations than the functional interests. The most that we can do with respect to the functional interests is to lump them together under three general headings. There are, first, those who are ideologically oriented and who are euphemistically referred to as the "cultural" elite. These involve the people who are in charge of the mass media, propaganda activities, theater, and all the other forms of political consciousness raising that the Chinese practice. Second, there are those who are involved in essentially industrial, managerial, and other "technocratic" administrative activities. Finally, there is the military. Much of the discussion in China does tend to revolve around the relative influence of these three groups with the first usually referred to as the "radicals," the second as the "moderates," and of course the third, simply the "military."

Much of the mystery in Chinese politics, however, deals with the more refined patterns of coalition formation and factional struggles. People who have been watching China far more carefully than I have been able to spot various potential coalitions and factions. Interestingly the first identification of such groupings came within the military when William Whitson (1973) noted that the various field armies were remarkably self-contained units. Recruits were brought into the separate field armies and stayed there, and each of the field armies had its own officer corps and its own distinctive leadership elements. This apparently is true to a greater extent within the PLA than in any other major army in the world. The various Chinese field armies have very clear local identifications.

It might be noted in passing that one of the considerations that may have contributed to the fall of Teng Hsiao-p'ing was that he was the first civilian leader who successfully transferred field commanders from one army to another.

Much of the speculation about succession in China revolves around the question of how firm are the various coalitions across issue areas. Some scholars have noted that different coalitions tend to form with respect to different policy issues. I suppose that at present the prudent statement is that we do find clusterings, but not very clear ones as yet.

The political process is not taking place in an open context, and therefore it is exceedingly difficult to place relative weight on the importance of generations, functional interests, and issues. The phenomenon of generations, however, does get accentuated because of the unquestioned presence of a great man on top of the whole process.

We must pause for a moment to take note of the personal qualities of the extraordinary charismatic leader, Chairman Mao Tse-tung, who has in various ways decisively shaped the Chinese political process. Presumably we know something about the characteristics of charismatic leaders from the insights of Max Weber. Mao, however, has defied Weber's theories in ways that Weber did not foresee. Weber presumed that a charismatic leader would have to rely upon various lieutenants who in carrying out their tasks would increasingly routinize and institutionalize their roles and thus create a new form of authority that would replace that of the charismatic leader. What Weber did not understand, and what Mao clearly reflects, is that the charismatic personality must also be a narcissistic person who would not readily allow his authority to become institutionalized. A great charismatic leader cannot exist without the kind of narcissism that a Mao Tse-tung seems to have. A man with that kind of narcissism is simply not going to allow lieutenants to institutionalize their roles. Mao, in his own personality, impinged upon the authority of all those beneath him, and in the end he has abandoned all of them.

Although it is easy to recognize that Mao is a charismatic leader, it is not easy to further classify him according to the functional interests because he clearly identifies in varying degrees with all of them and with none of them. At one moment Mao has been seen as the champion of one cause or one faction, and then at the next moment he is the champion of another cause or another faction. During the Cultural Revolution, everyone thought of Mao as the radical revolutionary, but then with the end of the Cultural Revolution he identified with the military for awhile. Then of course there was the new relationship with the United States and Mao became associated with a policy of normalizing relations with the outside world and seeking steady industrial development at home. In short, Mao has been able to shift and to show different faces at different times. This, of course, is really the nature of a charismatic leader. We could not expect a charismatic leader to gain his authority if he didn't have such a capacity for ambivalence and for startling changes in policy and programs. Indeed, the whole success of Mao Tse-tung can be in part attributed to his extraordinary capacity, over a long history, to change his persona to fit different roles.

The one thing that Mao does represent is his own generation, and he seems to be clinging to it with a tenacity that has disrupted all hopes for a smooth transition to his successor. As a narcissistic man he seems to reject completely the notion of death. In a sense he continues to grope for immortality by denying the need for the creation of any arrangements for what is to follow him. Leaders can postpone the need to have a plan for tomorrow if they can be certain that they will still be around to cope with tomorrow. Yet, Mao is concerned with the future as we can see from his constant haranguing of youth and his worry about whether the great masses of the Chinese are still dedicated to the revolution. In terms of ideology, he understands the imperatives of "succession," but in terms of the actual transfer of power, he seems to still want to deny the inevitable.

At the risk of engaging in excessive psychologizing, I would like to spend a few more moments discussing Mao's personality as it relates to succession. It seems to me that one of the key features of Mao's personality that has contributed to his success as a charismatic leader and has determined the way in which he has handled issues is the fact that he has never made any enduring commitments to any person. He has been intensely sensitive to the emotions of others, but he has always guarded his own emotions. Therefore, he has never allowed personal commitments to impede his policy choices. Indeed, a central theme running through his life has been that of abandoning relationships. At the same time, it is noteworthy that Mao is hypersensitive to the possibility that emotions will wither and disappear; hence his exaggerated concerns about the maintenance of revolutionary fervor with the next generation of Chinese youth.

I suspect that Mao came to believe that human relationships don't last as a result of his experiences with his mother: Initially being given a tremendous amount of nurturance and support and then feeling abandoned by his mother when his sibling brother came along, he would sense rejection and grow to feel that nothing in life is permanent. At the same time Mao challenged and outwitted his father. Indeed, he made a monkey of his father. From this he would have learned that it was easy to challenge authority; yet at the same time he would realize that it was dangerous to allow one's self to be put into the role of the "father" because fathers are extremely vulnerable.

We have no accurate count on the number of children that Mao has sired, but of those children we can identify as his, nearly all have been abandoned. Because he was able to make such a fool of his own father, he has pulled back from playing the role of father to his own children. For a time, he seems to have chosen to play instead the more abstract role of being the "father" to the Chinese revolution. But even in this respect he has found difficulties. It is interesting that Mao seems to be quite conscious of the problems of being a "father." Early in 1975, shortly before the meeting of the Second Plenary of the Tenth Party Congress, Mao wrote a poem to Chou En-lai that was quite appropriately entitled "To Reveal One's True Feelings."

Loyal parents who sacrifice so much for the nation never fear the ultimate fate. Now that the country's become red, who will be its guardian?
Our mission unfinished may take a thousand years. The struggle tires us, our hair is gray. You and I, old friends, can we just watch our efforts be washed away?

This is an extraordinary poem that I think reflects quite clearly the mood of an old man who is beset with doubts about the problems of generations.

So we come now to the phenomenon of old men in power and the question of the general characteristics of gerontocracies.

Plato pointed out that politics should be reserved for old men who would have the wisdom and the dampened ambitions to deal humanely with power. Younger people should be assigned more exacting tasks where energy is called for. We should be careful to note that Plato's theory is applicable primarily to situations in which stress is given to experience and not necessarily to "traditional" societies. Indeed, in some traditional societies in which ascriptive considerations are given great weight, it is possible for exceedingly young people to come to power. Note how early people used to come to power in British politics as compared with today. On the other hand, where emphasis is given to experience in defining the qualities of leadership, then there is likely to be a biasing in favor of age. This is even true for revolutionary societies as we have just seen with respect to China, because those who participated in the key events of the revolution, such as the Long March, achieved certain ascriptive qualities that will be denied all others and thus they can have a lifetime claim to special treatment.

Once power is thought of as primarily an executive or managerial task, then the cards are stacked in favor of younger people because of the need for vitality and new blood. American politics, for example, is primarily a young man's game. The contrast with Asian politics is sharp. In Asia the notion is that the elite should have leisure—that when you get to the top you should be able to relax a bit. This is certainly true of Mao's style of reigning and ruling. Politics is not something that requires high levels of energy but rather careful thought and visionary perspectives on the future. Politics in Asia generally requires that a leader allow others to expend their energies while he reserves the right to intervene at critical junctures.

Interestingly enough, the politics of gerontocracy tends paradoxically to mute the immediate father-to-son generational strain. The American executive style is very much patterned on the model of the father-son clash, in which the top executive must assert his leadership over the challenge of a rising elite. The gerontocratic pattern is much more that of grandfather, father, and son relationships. Once three or four generations are mixed, strains tend to be reduced and the relationship between generations is muted and blended, for there can be various coalitions of generations. The clash is not between any two generations because each can appeal to others as potential allies.

A second feature of gerontocracies, particularly as we find them in Asia, is the universal acceptance of the idea that elderly people should have power regardless of their formal position. In China there is no pattern of retirement and in Japan exofficials continue to be a part of the system and wield influence as, for example, the *Genro* once did. In the United States expresidents, even before Nixon, and exmembers of the Cabinet dramatically lose power on leaving office and are only occasionally solicited for their advice and views. This contrast brings us to the question of how gerontocracies are able to mute the conflict between reverence for age and the presumed need for new blood and vitality. The art of politics in a gerontocracy involves among other things skill in utilizing the vitality of youth without allowing youth to have exaggerated visions of its own importance. In a gerontocracy old men have to figure out how to get young people to work hard while preserving power for themselves. The secret of course lies in the concept of paternalistic authority in which the leader provides nurturance and support for subordinates who in turn are dedicated to upholding the common interest with the hope that in time they too will be able to claim their share of paternalistic authority. There is thus an exchange between the leader and the followers in which the leader provides symbolic support for the followers while the followers hold the leader in reverence. While it may be shocking to suggest this, I do believe that China today, in spite of all of its revolutionary rhetoric, does have a highly paternalistic form of authority.

Paternalism and gerontocracy do require not only a reverence for the aged, but also respect for the past. Again, paradoxically for a revolutionary society, China today does stress its revolutionary past and idealizes those who participated in the Long March. No small part of Mao's power and Mao's magic comes from the fact that the masses of Chinese people have been taught that they should revere the past and in a sense look backward. The source of his wisdom is in part based on the fact that he has experienced events that no one else has or can. This wisdom in turn is a source of tremendous power since it is the mystique that old men can use on young ones.

There is more to the mystique of age, however. We have to ask why it is that there seems to be a human tendency to respect the aged. I suspect that the almost universal tendency to recognize some element of piety for old people has to do with the awareness that the old are closer to death and therefore they tap upon the awe that all people have for the uncertainty of what goes with death. The contemplation of death usually creates anxiety and a sense that one should be willing to express some form of awe. Old men who are closer to death can consciously or unconsciously exploit the paralyzing effects that the awareness of death has for most people.

This linking of the mysteries of death with power and authority can be seen in the practices of nearly all religions. The shadow that death casts can strengthen the mystique of authority because of the deep ambivalences that we all feel about death. On the one hand, it is repugnant and something that we do not want to think about, and yet on the other hand, we all feel some need to be comforted with respect to death. In many religions, the kind of authority that is generated by ritual provides the psychological basis for coping with the mixed feelings about death. Old political leaders can also provide a form of reassurance: As long as the older generation is around, death is not imminent for the younger generation, and reverence for age can provide a way of postponing the inevitable for the self.

What all this points to is the fact that in a gerontocracy, authority rests upon a concept of legitimacy in which reverence for the past and the mystique of death play a very large part. Today we have in China a gerontocracy in which the legitimacy of the senior figure is in no sense challenged. Indeed, his legitimacy is so great that there is a tremendous sense of the impropriety of contemplating how the succession problem should be handled. Politically there is a sense of paralysis as everyone awaits the inexorable aging of Chairman Mao. The very act of discussing the inevitability of Mao's death can be seen as a form of plotting and scheming that brings with it a sense of profound illegitimacy. Nobody can openly jockey for position, yet everybody knows that the succession must take place.

In time, power will be transferred and the succession will take place. The big issue in China, however, is whether the next leadership will continue the tradition of gerontocracy and maintain the orderly layering of the political generations that were a part of the Chinese revolution, or whether there will be a genuine revolution and the ending of gerontocracy in China. Mao's China has ideologically upheld the virtues of youth, yet it has clung to the concept of paternalistic authority. Thus, Mao's China, like Confucius' China, looked to the past for its sources of legitimacy. Today, in China, there is as much respect and reverence for the authority of the aged as there was in Confucian China. If in the process of succession China should break out of the mold of a gerontocracy, then the scene would be set for a genuinely competitive politics of a profoundly revolutionary nature in Chinese civilization. Every indication, however, is that the mystique of age will continue to be used as the basis for upholding authority. In short, China is likely to have for some time a continuing politics of generations and a form of gerontocracy.

Discussion

Powell:

Let me ask a brief factual question. What is the age distribution in China today?

Pye:

I can't be absolutely accurate here, but I can say that China has a very young population. In societies in which very few people become old men, old men are valued items. There is still an element of that in China. Chinese culture was built around the notion that if anybody could live to be sixty, he should be held in awe. But in terms of demographic statistics, I think that something like one half of the population is under the age of fifteen. It is a tremendously young population.

Field:

Let me ask you to elaborate a bit on a comment you made. You spoke of legitimacy as if there is at the present time a crisis of legitimacy in China. When we think about legitimacy, we usually think about the attitudes that people have concerning the basic norms of a regime. Yet, in your comments you seemed to be referring to the question of personalities and figures very much in terms of succession. The question therefore arises, do you see in the unsettled question of succession some sort of impact on the more basic institutional question of legitimacy? This is the question of the regime as an ongoing entity quite apart from the identity of particular leaders at a particular point in time.

Pye:

It seems to me that until now the ultimate test of legitimacy in China has been the thoughts of Chairman Mao. What is striking in terms of the succession crisis that is developing is that Mao quite clearly has refused to make a commitment to anybody. He has not defined how that crisis is to be resolved. He did do this a couple of times in the past. It did appear for a while that Liu Shao-ch'i was going to succeed Mao. It appeared even more clearly in the case of Lin Piao, who was Mao's heir apparent and closest comrade in arms. But the ways in which these choices worked themselves out confirms the psychological problems that I've referred to. The more that Lin Piao tried to assert his claim as legitimate heir, the more Mao came to reject him, just as he came to reject his biological children. Mao has abandoned his wife, Chiang Ching, and thus the radicals attached to her are left without his blessing.

Mao is the old man who is unable to make any commitment of affect. Whenever he contemplates that commitment, he seems to recognize that whoever it is is unworthy. This is a difficult problem for most societies. But what complicates the Chinese case is the nature of the double bind they find themselves in. They've allowed themselves to go down the road where the old man is considered to be correct in all his statements. No one can contradict him. Yet, this is also a man whose greatness is partially based upon his inability to make a commitment to somebody else.

Field:

The question remains whether or not the basic values, orientations, and structuring of China since the revolution is in any sense in jeopardy, given Mao's
inability to determine his successor. If we believe fundamentally in the power of
the individual, we would say that these questions are up in the air. If we believe
in the significance of institutions and the durability of institutional arrangements, we would say that Mao, at this point, is a figurehead, while others hold
the effective reins of power. The system would go on, and the power struggles
will sort themselves out within the institutionalized system.

Pye:

I think that you've polarized the issue much too sharply. Of all the actors who
are being manipulated by Mao, none would abandon these institutional arrangements. What I am saying is that there is going to be a politics of succession in
China that Mao can't resolve for himself and that will produce a power struggle.
I'm not saying that the communist system will collapse. You can be certain
that the People's Republic of China will endure. This issue runs deeper than
the legitimacy of the system, in the sense that within a legitimate system you
may come to find a leader who himself cannot command legitimacy.

Huntington:

The problem appears at base to be that in the past the Chinese had these struggles for power, but they have all ultimately been resolved by Mao. When Mao is
gone, who is going to be around to play this moderator role, and who is going
to be able to establish a claim to authority? Whoever it is may have to produce
a secret last testament of Mao that will identify him as legitimate. There may
in fact be several of these produced by competitors.

    The other possibility may be that there will be a revulsion against this sort
of thing. In other words, we can ask, what will be the status of Mao in the
Chinese system five to ten years after his death? Will he be turned against? Will
someone deliver a speech at a party congress on the crimes of Chairman Mao?

Pye:

I assume that this is a case much closer to Lenin's than to Stalin's. Mao's mystique will be used by whoever follows for whatever purpose. The beauty of Mao
as a charismatic leader and father of his country is that he has made wise statements that can be used to support almost any contention. It's not unlike folk
mythology in this respect. Thus, anyone can mobilize the thoughts of Mao for

his own ends. Nobody has to destroy Mao; nobody has to do what Khrushchev did to Stalin. Quite the opposite is true. He is very available for all to use, in terms of contradictions. He is a man who enjoys contradictions and who confuses contradictions with the dialectic. Thus, he has said things that almost any successor could use, whatever that person's course might be.

So Mao will continue. But if you ask me if he will continue as the sacred figure that he is today, I would suspect not. The Chinese have almost no capacity for reverence. There is instead a great capacity for adapting to a new ruler.

Griffith:

The Soviet analogy is very dangerous, for what Mao has done is declare that the *party* can become corrupt—that the apparat must be overthrown. You are quite right. Mao has said things that Lenin would never have thought to say and that are potentially far more subversive for his successors than anything Lenin or Stalin ever said.

Pye:

We have long wondered why the Chinese have produced four volumes of Mao's selected works while they have not brought out his collected works. It seems quite clear that they never will. To do that would be to undercut any successor.

Sacks:

Powerholders will always decide what is appropriate and what is not appropriate when it comes to using the writings of a past, great leader. This has always been the case. There is no question of the right interpretation, for the right interpretation belongs to the wielder of power. What concerns me is the methodological problem here. You make an excellent description of Mao as a person and in terms of what he means to the Chinese system, but you don't fully treat the problem of the role of gerontocracy. It is one thing to discuss how the gerontocratic approach can make Mao a particular kind of figure in China. But there is another issue. Suppose that at the time Lin Piao was the designated heir there had been a natural catastrophe that befell Mao. Would Lin Piao have been accepted at that time?

Pye:

It seems to me that the passage of power would have been much easier. If Mao had died just after the Ninth Party Congress, Lin Piao would have stepped in quite easily.

Hogue:

I'd like to pursue the question of the passage of power. I think we're agreed that there is no rock upon which the change will be made. What I'd really like to have your view on is just what is going to happen when the day comes when Mao dies? Is there a system for the passage of power, particularly in the long term? If there is no system, what do you suspect is going to happen?

Pye:

I think that most analysis is focused on the larger dimensions of the issues, like the struggle between the pragmatists who are running the economy and the ideologues who will uphold the revolution. I'm sure that these are very important issues, but if you ask me to focus on the more intimate issue that you suggest, I think that you do come down to the one issue that may in fact decide an awful lot—that is, who is going to control the body of the chairman? Who is going to govern the ceremony? What ritual will be performed, and who decides that? You can't bury this body without engaging in certain kinds of rituals. This is what is being jockeyed for; they don't want the warm body, they want the cold body.

He has obviously abandoned his wife Chiang Ching, but he hasn't divorced her. Thus, she does still have some claim on this. She has claims that go far beyond her actual political power. The other side can look toward the institutional arrangements and say that their way is how it should be done. I'm amazed that there hasn't been more speculation as to how they will inter this man. For better or for worse, I think these decisions have already been made. I think that he's going to be buried right within the Forbidden City. I think that neither side will get any benefit from his body.

Huntington:

When you say neither side, which are the two sides that you're referring to?

Pye:

I think that in this sense identification is no problem. There are two basic sides and there is a third dimension. One side is made up of the combination of people that Chou En-lai was trying to pass power to. These are the "Ivy Leaguers," the white-shoe boys of the system. These are in fact embarassingly few people, including a group of Shanghai-type, foreign cultured sophisticates who have been nurtured and carefully protected. So much capital has been expended in protecting these people, that they must come to have power in the end.

The opposition is comprised of the ideologues who are very much identified with the mass media and Chiang Ching, Mao's wife. Thus, the struggle will be between those currently identified with the propaganda machinery and those who deal with substantive policy. Both have an organizational base. The strain is the old and ubiquitous one between form and substance. On the side, of course, is the military. Mao has been remarkably successful, more so than most people would have expected, in cutting down the military. Yet obviously they still have the arms and are capable of reentering the arena.

Howells:

I'd like to return to the poem that you have included. If Mao wrote that poem, what do you think the chances are that there is another legacy that has not yet been unveiled.

Pye:

I think that it is a tradition in Chinese society to leave a will. Sun Yat-sen left a will. Certainly Mao will do the same. This is something that will be jockeyed over. But look at how Stalin handled what Lenin left. I think that if the will goes against Mao's eventual successor, it will undoubtedly be suppressed. There are so many other things written by Mao that can legitimate his successors that a will could easily be suppressed.

But, I can put this issue in another way. Mao's problem would more likely be that he cannot decide on the content of his will: Psychologically, he is unable to write one, for he is a man for whom the act of writing a will entails engaging in something that he doesn't want to think about—his own death. When he does write one, it will be written under very bizarre circumstances. He's had his chance to write his will. He could have written it some time ago. Every time he attempts to set up his successor, he undercuts that person.

Rangarajan:

I am reminded by this discussion of what happened in Vietnam after the death of Ho Chi-Minh. There a collegiate body succeeded a charismatic figure. But they had a distinctive factor that unified them, a common enemy. In the face of a common enemy it is easier to bridge some of these major differences. So, I wonder if Mao is setting up the Soviet Union as this sort of common enemy that could serve to unify his successors to make possible a collegiate rule of China after his death. Why is he pursuing this anti-Soviet line? Is it for this reason?

Pye:

Mao has the grounds for a deep resentment toward the Soviet Union. You can go back to 1927 and find a long history of the ways in which the Soviets hurt the Chinese communists. What is absolutely fascinating is that Mao has never publicly come out against Stalin. He has never really damned those Soviet acts that he legitimately could have. In fact, Stalin is the only person, except for the father of his first wife, who Mao has ever fully accepted as his superior. It would have been so easy for Mao to have made the jump from Marx and Engels to Lenin to himself and leave out Stalin entirely. But he hasn't. Yet at the same time, I would agree with you that the bitterness toward the Soviet Union is excessive. The degree to which he is preoccupied by his fear that the Soviets are going to cause war is excessive.

Field:

The question of the succession in China sounds very much like a squabble in a geriatric ward. It is not clear who among the lieutenants, all of whom are almost as old as Mao, is really to be annointed. The point then becomes that whatever the outcome of the squabble, it probably wouldn't have an enduring significance. So one must wonder about the way in which the Chinese system goes about the recruiting of new blood. How are the younger potential leaders given a connection to those who dwell in the geriatric ward? Is there any evidence that leads you to believe that the politics of the geriatric ward are not terribly important and that things are going on outside this sanctum that in the longer run might be of much greater consequence?

Pye:

In a strange kind of way China, not unlike Indonesia, is a very easy country to run. But the politics of being at the top is very tough and has almost no connection with the running of the country. The system is very well entrenched. Where the Chinese elite will have difficulty is when it has to make command decisions, when it has to shift from one set of priorities to another. Short of that, there is a structure for agriculture, for industry, and so on. The Chinese system is not like the one in the United States where a lot of decisions have to be referred to the president. In the Chinese system very few decisions are made at the top of the structure, which thus makes it possible for Mao to practice his extraordinary act of ruling and reigning.

This is not to imply that there is no dissent in China. There *are* big issues, but they get muted on the way to the top. The Chinese system has problems, but Mao in part has created something called "the center." Nobody quite knows what it is, but all Chinese talk in terms of it. What is fascinating is that while Mao has been opposed to bureaucracy and abstract authority, he has created this most abstract of authorities. So, while all sorts of issues evolve toward the center, when the center says something, it is almost like divine guidance, nobody challenges it. He has diffused the whole idea, and Mao is two steps above the center.

Endo:

As far as the eminent figures of Chinese politics are concerned, most come from the days of the Long March. In this light, what is the significance of each of the other generations that you've outlined? What is the nature of the cleavages among these generations? How will these cleavages affect the succession struggle?

Pye:

Here we are dealing with something very much like the differences among college graduating classes. The party apparatus operates in such a way that promotions are determined very much by seniority. So, the anti-Japanese War generation represents the senior cadres. These are the men who hold very important offices. Anyone who came into the party after the surrender, with only a few exceptions, is down below. The man who joined the party after 1949 is in yet a much humbler position. I should have mentioned that this was part of the Cultural Revolution. One of the beauties of the notion of retirement is not getting rid of dead wood, but rather loosening up things within a bureaucracy so that promotion is made possible. This problem is very much with the Chinese: They don't know how to puncture the ceiling to allow for promotion. They haven't demonstrated an ability to provide for a succession to the generation of the Long March.

Huntington:

You've indicated that the different generations in China are self-conscious generations, that they think of themselves as being distinct. This leads then to two other questions: Are there other significant differences among these generations in addition to their differences in age? For example, are there identifiable differences in outlook or policy? Secondly, can you have generational differences without necessarily having generational conflict?

Pye:

In answer to your first question, I think we can identify differences among generations other than in terms of age in the sense of the promotional pattern. What has happened is that the anti-Japanese War generation is still down at the level of the colonels, and they want to become generals. The problem is in picking only some of them, because then there would be problems with the others. But we really can't speak of differences in terms of their outlook, that is, of some within a given generation being more or less hostile to the USSR or more or less prone to support Third World causes than others within that generation. The problem is that these officials are so absolutely faceless. Take a look at Teng Hsiao-ping's toast to President Ford. You can't find a single sentence, a single word that is not a direct quote from Chairman Mao. He ran together phrase after phrase that are directly attributable to Mao. So, if you ask me what Teng Hsiao-ping's view is, I would find it very hard to cite any evidence that he has ever made one public.

Hogue:

Along these same lines, is it possible to identify more broadly than you already have any distinction between the generation that remembers 1949 and the generation now in their twenties and thirties that does not? Are there differences between those who have not known anything but the glories of the People's Republic and those who can remember the evil days before 1949?

Pye:

If you ask this in a precise sense, what is interesting is that almost everything we've learned about what has been going on sociologically within China points toward the fact that in many ways there has been a freezing of relationships. For example, the pattern of rural to urban migration has been cut off. So the normal change in people's attitudes that comes from cityward migration has been eliminated. The fact is that people have been sent from the city back to the countryside. In terms of very detailed studies of families and villages, what is extraordinary is that the grandparents' generation is closer to the sons than are the fathers. In part this is because both husband and wife are working and thus the children are being reared by the grandparents. Children are closer to the world of their grandparents than they are to the world of their parents.

Secondly, what seems to be happening is that the tendency toward functional specialization that went with a lot of rituals such as burials, weddings, and religion is being reversed. Instead of one wise man, one specialist in a village, now everyone is capable of performing these tasks. The rituals still take place, but now everyone takes part in them. The maintenance of tradition has been strengthened precisely because the specialists have been eliminated.

References

Barnett, Doak A. 1967. *China After Mao*. Princeton, N.J.: Princeton University Press.

Dahl, Robert A. 1962. *Who Governs?* New Haven, Conn.: Yale University Press.

Hunter, Floyd. 1953. *Community Power Structure*. Chapel Hill: University of North Carolina Press.

Whitson, William W. (ed.). 1973. *The Military and Political Power in China in the 1970s*. New York: Praeger.

10 Generational Change and Political Leadership in Eastern Europe and the Soviet Union

William E. Griffith

There has been much debate recently in the field of communist studies concerning whether or not it is really a viable field. Many have wondered whether we might not better deal with the Soviet Union and Eastern Europe as part of a field that focuses on developed industrial societies, such as East Germany, or as part of a field that focuses on the politics of less-developed societies, as in parts of Yugoslavia and the USSR, for example. I am not certain to what extent the argument has itself developed, but it does point up the fact that this is an enormously variegated area. There is really very little that is common to it, except for the existence in each case of a centralized elite rule possessing fairly consistent ideological elements. I will argue, however, first in relation to the Soviet Union and then in relation to Eastern Europe, that aspects of (a) tradition, (b) hierarchy, (c) the lack of any legitimate and regularized pattern of succession, and (d) the nature of absolute power all serve to slow down generational change.

The result of this pattern in the Soviet Union is the creation of a gerontocracy. The outcome of the Twenty-Fifth Party Congress was an increase in the average age of the Politburo and of the Central Committee. The average ages of both have been steadily increasing ever since Stalin died. In the past, of course, there have been phenomena, such as the great purge of the 1930s, that rapidly increased generational mobility. If a leader kills twenty million people, as Stalin did in one way or another, a lot of opportunities are created for younger careerists. Indeed, these are the young men who are now in power in the Soviet Union. Brezhnev, Kosygin, Podgorny, and Suslov, among others, "walked over corpses," to use a German phrase. They rose rapidly because their competitors were killed.

In the case of the Soviet Union, we can find three generations. There is first the gerontocracy, that is, the leadership of the Politburo, of the military, and of the police. Secondly, we can find a middle generation of people who are either in their forties or fifties. Finally, we can find the youth, or people under thirty years of age.

Let me begin with the youth. In the Soviet Union, as in much of Eastern Europe, there is far less differentiation between "under thirty" and "over thirty" than there is in the West. Neither a youth culture nor a politicized youth culture exists to the extent it does in Western societies. This is true for several reasons; there is less privacy, less affluence, and infinitely more police control. The elite is recruited largely via the Komsomol, the communist youth

125

organization, from among people whom we would think of as the "big men on campus." These are the people who rise to party positions. But the fact of the gerontocracy precludes the entrance of the younger elites into positions of real power. The procedure is much slower than it is in the West. We can think of this in terms of the example of the *chinovniki*, the Russian civil servant characterized by obscurantism, illiteracy, and incompetence. The *chinovniki* largely still dominate. Russia is still run by the *chinovniki*.

The middle generation is more educated and more technocratic than was its equivalent a generation ago. Indeed, we can say that in the generation of Khrushchev, leaders emerged through their participation in the revolution and the civil war. These people achieved their status before they acquired their education. Today, the middle generation acquires its status through education. This change is significant. However, the education is primarily that of engineering. Thus, there is the predominance of elites with a technological training and a technocratic outlook. We can then argue, using Khrushchev and Brezhnev as the two symbols, that the utopian aspects of the ideology have declined with generational progress. We can trace this change in the ideology by comparing Khrushchev's party program of 1961, which was concerned with the immediate transition to communism, with the current ideology of "scientific communism" in which communism is equated with high technology and rapid economic growth.

Perhaps in order to make this all a bit more specific, I should turn to the Russian political culture. Generational change is slowed down by the persistence of several traditional factors of Russian political culture. I say Russian, rather than Soviet, because it is Russian not only in terms of the empire, but also in terms of the Russian versus the minority nationalities. There is also the patrimonial aspect, which Richard Pipes (1974) has developed, that the rulers of Russia have always believed that they rightfully own not only the land, but the inhabitants of Russia. Another point that he has made in his new book, *Russia Under the Old Regime*, is that by the 1880s, Russia had become a state ruled by the police. Police power was briefly interrupted at the time of the Bolshevik revolution, but it was rapidly restored. Although mass terror does not exist in the Stalinist fashion, the elite continues to rule through the police.

Other aspects of the Russian political culture, which deserve mention as well, influence the rate of generational change. The first, which is in part a reflection of the role of the police, is the fact that the great mass of the population is genuinely apolitical. The people go through the rites and rituals of participation, just as they used to engage in the rites and rituals of the Orthodox Church. Nevertheless, it is fundamentally apolitical. Among the younger elites, there is a heavy dose of Sam Rayburn's advice to young congressmen: "Go along to get along."

This apolitical aspect comes in large measure also from a second element of

Russian political culture: the conviction of political impotence. There is the realization among the great mass of the population that it makes no difference what they do. They will continue to be dominated from above. The popular way to refer to the elite of the party is the Russian word *oni*, which means "they." "They" have always been different. "They" have always had power, privilege, and wealth, and today "they" have them to a greater degree than they did in Czarist Russia.

The third aspect of Soviet political culture is the modernizing aspect, which has involved, since Stalin, the expectation of a certain gradual improvement in the delivery by the regime of goods and services. Since the regime has been successful in keeping the population isolated from the West, the possibility for comparison is small. And since the regime's privileges are almost completely hidden, the comparison cannot readily be made here either.

Let me turn now to the problem of generational change among the non-Great Russians. I'll begin with the flat assertion that the nationality issue will be the central problem in the Soviet Union for the next generation. The other nations in the Soviet Union outside the Great Russians are about to become more than half the Soviet population. In these nations, I would argue, generational change is much more important because of the acceleration of the processes of education and modernization. There has been mass education, rapid economic growth, modernization, and thus inevitably rising nationalism. These changes increase discontent and thus increase the support within each passing generation of Great Russians for an autocratic regime dominated by Great Russians. It is only Great Russian domination that can maintain the USSR as a united and powerful state. If the Soviet Union were a democratic state, it would either collapse or be even more inhibited than Yugoslavia. Because the Great Russians are the more powerful half of the population, they are unlikely to relinquish their power. As part of their efforts to develop their Asian areas, the Soviets are moving Russian nationals into Soviet Asia. The largest Central Asian republic, Kazakhstan, is now less than one-half Kazaks. Siberia had been as empty as the United States and has long been settled by Great Russians.

I would argue that generational change will be most rapid in these modernizing areas of the Soviet Union. But I would also argue that such change will be continually and successfully suppressed by the Great Russian domination. There are institutional channels operating to enhance this suppression. Through the procedure of the *nomenklatura*, every important job is approved by a higher party level. It is not a Cold War cliche to say that the Soviet Union is the last great colonial power; it is the literal truth. We can also argue that in Soviet Central Asia we may see, in addition to modernization, a revival of Islam. I think that we will see this revival spread into Soviet Central Asia from the Arab World. But again, what we see is a sort of generational revolving door. Nationalism is constantly produced and is constantly purged.

I also should address the generational problem in the dissent movement, in *samizdat*. A certain element of this movement is made up of people whose fathers had been struck down in the great purges. Yakir and Litvinov are good examples. But these persons, however, were very few in number. I don't think that generational change is the key element in the *samizdat* movement. The movement is now in very low ebb. Its people have been either driven abroad, jailed, or otherwise silenced. I would argue that its greatest generational effect will be not upon the Great Russians, but upon the other nationalities.

I would like to conclude with respect to the Soviet Union on the problem of what is to become of the gerontocratic leadership. It was often thought, before the Twenty-Fifth Congress, that there would have to be a rejuvenation. But nothing of the sort has occurred. I would argue that the factors that I mentioned at the beginning remain operational and that the system tends to slow down the transition from one generation to the next. Indeed, it is likely to continue to do so.

Let me now turn to Eastern Europe. Again, let me note how difficult it is to speak of it as a unified region. East Germany is in central Europe, and Albania is part of the Middle East. We find here, to a greater extent than in the Baltic States, nationalism against communism and against the Soviet Union. Greatly different traditions exist with respect to Russia and Germany. Great differences exist between those communist parties that have had mass bases, as in the Czech lands, Bulgaria, and Germany, on the one hand, and those parties that were alienated sects as in Poland and Hungary, on the other hand.

One of the problems of generational change in Eastern Europe in those countries where communist parties were sects has been the problem of minority versus majority ethnicity. The Polish and Hungarian communist parties before 1945 were minuscule, illegal sects that were overwhelmingly composed of non-ethnic Poles and Magyars. In fact, they were overwhelmingly Jewish. In the case of Rumania, much the same was true; they were overwhelmingly Jewish, Ukranian, Hungarian, and Bulgarian. The key here is the nonmajority ethnicity within the leadership of these parties. This was also true in Yugoslavia where the prewar party was largely non-Serb. One of the reasons why this pattern continued was that until 1935 the Comintern insisted on the principle of self-determination to the point of separation. It seemed to be actively opposed to the unity of these countries.

What resulted under Stalin and his anti-Semitism and then afterwards with Khrushchev's "pragmatic" anti-Semitism was a rapid departure of the non-majority ethnics. Today, the Rumanian Politburo is overwhelmingly Rumanian, whereas before 1952 it was overwhelmingly not. Today there are practically no Jews left in the leadership of Poland and Hungary, whereas, in 1953, the only non-Jew in the Hungarian Politburo was Imre Nagy, which is why he became prime minister. The culmination of all of this was the anti-Semitic purge of 1968 in Poland. This purge has, I would argue, brought rapid generational change. It was initiated by its imposition by Stalin and Khrushchev and it was accelerated by the increasing power of the majority ethnics. The result has been in Poland, for example, particularly since Gomulka was removed, a regime that is largely in its fifties and much younger than the regime in the Soviet Union. The same is true in Rumania. The point, however, is that this seeming generational shift is most likely a temporary phenomenon as it was in the 1930s in the USSR. Now that the majority ethnics are in power, the phenomenon of the gerontocracy will reassert itself.

In terms of generational change, there is also, in Eastern Europe, an element of the kind of distinction between the technocrats and the party elite that I noted was the case in the Soviet Union. One of the few serious studies that has been done on this topic is the work by Ludz (1972) of the University of Munich. Ludz maintains that a counterelite had developed in East Germany before the fall of Ulbricht. This technocratic group of people was more interested in efficiency than in the more utopian aspects of party ideology. Clearly there has been the development of interest groups that are to some extent generational. But on the other hand, the political elite in a country like Hungary seems to have discovered a new role for itself. Some of the younger technocrats have tried to introduce a program of rationalization, some decentralization, and some elements of a market economy, which has seemed threatening to the unskilled working class. There has been a sort of a reaction within this unskilled working class that has been taken up by the generally older Hungarian bureaucrats in the party and trade union leadership.

In the case of Yugoslavia, the most special of all cases, the generational issue is distorted by the fact that Tito is so old. So too, the movement of nationalism and liberalism in Zagreb in 1971 was younger. The then secretary of the Croat party, Mika Tripalo, was in his early forties as was Savka Dapcevic-Kucar. Indeed, it was largely student based. Yugoslavia has not had genuine generational change, although there has been a rejuvenation that Tito has, in a way, artificially prevented from coming to fruition. I would suspect that there is, in Yugoslavia, a great deal of builtup generational resentment.

Generally speaking, Eastern Europe has less of a gerontocracy than the Soviet Union for the reasons I presented initially. It may well be, however, that after the current ethnic circulation of cadres, the tendency will be toward more of a gerontocracy and the pattern of Soviet leadership in the post-Stalinist period.

Discussion

Haviland:

I would like to hear a bit more about the dissident intellectuals. It seems to me that the greatest threat to the authoritarian regimes of Eastern Europe and the USSR are the intellectuals. They are becoming increasingly more sophisticated and more cosmopolitan. I am sure that, in the long run, they will come to challenge these regimes.

Griffith:

I cannot agree with you on this point. The intellectuals lose their cohesiveness as modernization proceeds. They separate into the creative intelligensia, which is alienated just as you have described, and into the technocratic intelligentsia, which goes along with the regime precisely because it is favored. Indeed, this second group is increasingly favored as modernization takes place. The creative intellectuals are very much alienated, but they are either bought out, thrown out, locked up, or otherwise taken care of. These dissidents, in my opinion, have done more than one would have expected, but their effect has been practically destroyed. That it has lasted so long is probably because Brezhnev and, earlier, Khrushchev thought that it would be counterproductive to shoot them all. I can assure you that if they were convinced they had to shoot them all, they would do so immediately. Since the mass of the population is proud of its achievements, fearful of the non-Great Russians, scared of the Chinese, and skeptical about the Americans, I regret to say that I don't anticipate the kind of challenge you envision.

Huntington:

Your comments have suggested to me that we can think of two different types of regimes in relation to generational succession. There is first the modern autocratic regime with its long-lived gerontocratic regime, in which there is a conscious promotion of younger people. A source of its power is its ability to introduce younger generations to rule. The best example, perhaps, is the monarchy with its regularized pattern of succession. The second type is that of the modern democratic state in which, in one sense, generational differences may be much more important. There is a sense of younger politicians and their cohorts challenging more senior leaders in the Congress, in local politics, and elsewhere. It seems to me that one interesting question, in terms of the Soviet Union, is how significant is the generational cleavage as contrasted to other lines of cleavage. You've mentioned the cleavages of nationality, of region, and of institution. I infer from what you've said that there is very little, if any, generational consciousness or generational cleavage in the USSR.

Griffith:

I would think that there is some consciousness, but that it is not terribly important. It is not important because the day-to-day control of the central gerontocratic leadership is maintained by the institution of the *nomenklatura*. Every important position, in any aspect of Soviet life, has to be approved by a higher party office. For example, the Prime Minister of the Ukrainian Republic would have to be approved by the Central Committee in Moscow. There is, thus, a vast centralized personnel system. There is also the vast police system; there are two systems of intelligence: the military and the KGB. The *nomenklatura* works through all of that too. In short, the *nomenklatura* keeps generational conflict under control.

Huntington:

There is a certain amount of evidence that suggests that in noncommunist autocratic regimes, there are generational groupings in the army as determined perhaps by the common experience of a cohort group in the military academy, for example. These are more than categorical groups, for they often represent discrete political groups as well. I take it that there is very little evidence of anything of this sort in the Soviet Union.

Griffith:

That may be because we know so little about it. But there has been a striking rejuvenation of the Soviet military leadership. People who are now quite highly placed in the military are in their fifties. In this regard, also, personal ties are quite important. We might say then that cliques and factions run vertically, and not horizontally, in terms of status and age.

Dominguez:

What is striking about the Soviet case is not merely that gerontocracy has taken hold, but that a particular type of gerontocracy has evolved. It is really a bureaucratic gerontocracy. It does not rely upon a charismatic figure like Tito, nor upon a traditionally legitimate person like a monarch. What seems unique is that it is a gerontocracy of a bureaucratic sort. This pattern also seems plausible in Eastern Europe, with the exception of Yugoslavia and Albania, where single leaders seem important.

Griffith:

The Marxist-Leninist myth has always worked in this direction. It has always talked of the collective wisdom of the Central Committee. In the case of Eastern Europe you are certainly correct about Yugoslavia and Albania, although these cannot endure indefinitely. But you are wrong about Rumania. Rumania today has the greatest cult of the personality anywhere in the world outside China.

The patterns are somewhat more bureaucratized in the rest of Eastern Europe, as you suggest. But I don't see any reason why this should be fixed. I would agree with Max Weber that the Ice Age of bureaucracy needs charismatic leaders.

Field:

Wouldn't you agree that there is a certain incentive for the assertion of charisma when the charisma is really a way of expressing national defiance?

Griffith:

Yes, indeed. Tito and Ceausescu are examples. Brezhnev's cult of the personality is minor in comparison, although it does exist and it is increasing.

Sacks:

What is important with respect to generational change is the thrust upward of younger, emerging leaders and their conflict with their senior rulers. I am very much taken with the fact that, for the first time, it is being asserted that contrary to what we usually hear about communist systems, there are no apparent succession crises. I would argue that the mechanism of collectivity serves to preclude generational transfer.

Griffith:

I would agree, but I would suggest that it is always possible that there would be a succession struggle, as there was after Stalin's death. It is interesting that the people disposed of by Brezhnev, such as Shelepin, have all been in their fifties. In a sense then, the gerontocracy has been reinforced.

Weiner:

I find a curious difference in the generational element between the case of China and the case of the Soviet Union. In one sense, they are similar in that they both have a gerontocracy. But the fundamental difference is that in the Chinese case one element of the gerontocracy sees itself as potentially allied with the younger generation. In the Soviet case, the older generation has no desire to ally itself with the youth. I suppose one difference is that the Soviet party sees itself as the party of the whole people, whereas the Chinese party sees itself as the party of the class struggle, as the defender of a continuing revolution. From the Chinese perspective, the way to preserve the revolutionary spirit is to reach down beyond the bureaucratized middle-aged groups to the youth.

Griffith:

I would emphasize here the role of Mao personally. He disposed one after the other of persons in his age group. It does appear that the Chinese pattern has differed from the Soviet pattern, and indeed it is unique in communist history, in that there is a belief by Mao in the inevitable degeneracy of communist systems. Thus, it is a thrust for a permanent revolution not before communism, as Trotsky maintained, but within communism in order to dispose of entrenched bureaucrats.

I would rather doubt that after Mao dies there will be a sort of institutionalization of noninstitutionalization. The contrary is much more likely. We must remember that Mao is practically Marx, Lenin, Trotsky, and Stalin all in the same person.

Huntington:

I'd like to return to a theme that figured prominently in your remarks, the nationality issue. You suggested that this issue is going to be the major problem for the next generation in the Soviet Union. I'm impressed with the frequency with which I've heard that prediction over the years. What has changed in the last decade or so that makes it more important in the 1980s and 1990s than it was in the 1950s and 1960s. Is it because there are more educated people within these nationalities than before? To what extent is there emerging a new generation of nationalist leaders among the Kazaks, the Georgians, and the rest?

Griffith:

As I noted, the nationality issue will be the great domestic problem in the USSR for precisely the reasons you've stated: more modernization, more education, more nationalism. But these leaders can be eliminated by the machinery that is presently available. I should point out that we know that the *samizdat* movement is far more serious among some of these nationalities—the Ukrainians and Lithuanians, for example—than it is among the Great Russians. The number of arrests in these areas is higher.

Dominguez:

Let me try to present a defense of gerontocratic rule. Such a defense would take two forms. First, it can be argued that a gerontocracy is necessary for stability. Nelson Polsby (1968) advanced this argument in his description of the seniority system in the U.S. House of Representatives. The second related argument, which would hold that gerontocracy is appropriate for the Soviet system, suggests that where other mechanisms for succession are not institutionalized, gerontocratic rule remains the only legitimate alternative. So, we could make the twofold argument for gerontocracies that, first, it is a source of stability in many political organizations and that, secondly, in the case of the USSR, it offers the only recourse to legitimate rule.

Griffith:

I entirely agree with you that, in terms of legitimacy and stability, age is the only alternative. There is no other way to handle it in the Soviet Union.

Weiner:

I would like to return to an argument that has emerged again and again in our discussions—that of the importance of critical formative events and experiences that shape the political orientations of individuals and groups. Can we look at a sample of communist leaders and find some common formative experiences?

Griffith:

It is quite clear that in the Soviet Union for Khrushchev, the experience was the Bolshevik Revolution, and for Brezhnev it was the great purge. For Mao, it was clearly Yenan and the Civil War.

References

Ludz, Peter C. 1972. *The Changing Party Elite in East Germany*. Cambridge, Mass.: MIT Press.

Pipes, Richard. 1974. *Russia Under the Old Regime*. London: Weidenfeld and Nicholson.

Polsby, Nelson. 1968. "The Institutionalization of the U.S. House of Representatives," *American Political Science Review*, vol. 62, no. 1 (March), pp. 144–68.

11

Conclusion: The Politics of Age

Jorge I. Dominguez

The discussion of political generations has left us with a great deal of consensus as well as much disagreement on the topic. A part of the disagreement results primarily from the variety of country settings considered. A part of the agreement may have resulted from the deference of the participants to the topic. Asked to discuss a subject, social scientists will often manage to say something. The purpose of this concluding chapter is to attempt to sort out the substantive from the accidental in our consensus and disagreements.

Every author in this volume agrees that age matters for politics at least some of the time. There are, however, disagreements about how important the politics of age are, what difference they make, how lasting they are, and what sorts of generational explanations are appropriate. Some areas of possible agreement were not fully discussed. On other items concerning the politics of age, many participants in the discussion would probably be in agreement on their importance.

The politics of age are especially relevant to certain issues, such as schools for the young and pensions and medical care for the old. The actors concerned about these issues are often defined, in important ways, in terms of age: parents, students, old people, young taxpayers affected by social security, and so forth. Because the discussion was structured principally along country or area lines, these issues did not receive much attention, although students were frequently mentioned.

The politics of age are especially relevant in highly institutionalized organizations. Military institutions often recruit and promote in terms of age. Stepan's discussion of the armed forces in Latin America, principally in Brazil and Peru, highlights this issue well. Certain political parties have also recruited and promoted in terms of age. Perlmutter's discussion of Israel, Pye's on China, and Griffith's on Eastern Europe and the Soviet Union all indicate the importance of age for these political parties and, indeed, more generally for those entire political systems. Although churches were not explicitly considered, clearly some—such as the Roman Catholic Church—can also be analyzed in terms of the politics of age. University faculties and both public and private bureaucracies exhibit similar features.

These remarks suggest that the politics of age may be especially appropriate to understand certain kinds of political systems, although the actual content of these politics would differ. None of the authors of this volume contends that generational variables should override consideration of other variables. We seek not to reduce the stock of tools in the social science tool kit, but to add to it.

135

Thus one important intellectual task is to attempt to point to relationships between age and other variables. When is it that the study of the politics of age may add substantially to our understanding? In what ways may age-related variables interact with other variables? The following paragraphs can be considered hypotheses for further work along the lines suggested in this volume.

First, relatively traditional political systems on the edge of modernizing change may be strongly affected by the politics of age through the action of students. Social, economic, and political organizations in these kinds of political systems may not yet be strongly differentiated and articulated. The number of political participants is relatively small and concentrated in the urban areas of largely agrarian societies. The first effects of modernization probably lowered the mortality rate, with little change in the birth rate, and thus created a large and relatively youthful population. University and high school students tend to be a disproportionately large share of the politically active and capable population. They are defined principally by their positions in the age structure; they are conscious of their roles as students; and they often communicate with each other and act politically. The studies by Isaacs and Quandt, and Huntington's reference to Venezuela, provide examples of these phenomena.

Second, political systems that were founded in some way may be strongly affected by the politics of age in a variety of ways (see especially Huntington's chapter on the United States). Some societies may be founded through large-scale immigration; most of the contemporary developing countries, however, do not fit this description. Some political systems may have been founded by political action, and several of those studied in this book fit this category. In the chapters by Isaacs, Weiner, Pye, Griffith, Quandt, and Perlmutter, this set of issues is highlighted. There was a founding generation, which came to power either upon a revolution, or after colonial withdrawal, or both. Their eventual displacement or more peaceful replacement—or the difficulty in accomplishing either—became major political problems. Because these founders gave their country's politics such a clear age dimension, their challengers and successors often came to be age defined.

Third, the importance of the politics of age in founded political systems varies according to the degree of institutionalization of organizations and procedures. The more important and institutionalized these are, the more important the politics of age will be. Thus Pye discusses four layered generations in China with a degree of content and specificity that is a bit more difficult for Quandt and Isaacs to do. One key difference may be the role of political organizations; only in Isaacs' (and Weiner's) discussion of India can one approximate the age specificity that Pye (and Griffith) describe for the countries they study.

Fourth, political systems where the armed forces play an important role in politics are also shaped strangely by the politics of age, although in two quite different ways. If the armed forces are accustomed to short interventions in political affairs, followed by relatively swift withdrawal, the interactive model of the politics of age (see the chapters by Huntington and Samuels) is likely to be most important. Different age groups linked to military rank within the armed forces may compete for power and influence. If the armed forces have seized power and have ruled themselves for a substantial period of time, then the experiential model that is characteristic of the previous hypotheses is likely to prevail. Stepan's work sheds light on these issues.

Fifth, very modern societies may be strongly affected by the politics of age as predicted by the maturation or life cycle. In these societies, the birth rate has fallen rapidly, so that the young population is much smaller; the formerly young, however, are still making their way through middle and old age. The numbers of old people become much larger than ever before; their concern with pensions, medical care, housing for the elderly, and related issues is shaped by their position in the life cycle. These politics may be, of course, more characteristic of Europe, North America, and East Asia than of other societies.

Sixth, political systems where political conflicts along class or communal (ethic, racial, religious, regional) lines are perceived to be illegitimate may be far more susceptible to the politics of age. The inability to organize politically on a sustained basis along these other lines may induce people to organize politically along generational lines. This appears to have happened in the countries studied by Pye and Griffith.

The first and fifth hypotheses identified above suggest that the politics of age may be especially pertinent in societies on the edge of a major transition—either from relatively traditional to modernizing politics, or from modern industrial politics of postindustrial, service society politics. The issues in the politics of age, and their consequences, are obviously quite different in these transitions. But each major transition in the basic characteristics of the economy and the society may be associated with a major change in demographic structure. The interaction of these major changes also appears to have an effect on politics. More generally, a study of the politics of age serves to cut across societies at various points on the developmental spectrum. Unlike some variables (e.g., the spread of literacy) that are applicable only to a certain kind of society for a specific part of its history, the politics of age are apparently important to many more different kinds of societies for several parts of their history. In short, although the politics of age are basically concerned with developmental questions—change, time, continuity—they are not peculiar to underdeveloped, developing, or developed countries. Thus this is a developmental variable that is not of exclusive interest to students of one type of country, but to a broader set of scholars and countries.

The authors in this volume have also identified a variety of circumstances when the politics of age are likely to be less important, although they focused on this part of the argument a good deal less. It is, however, also our collective responsibility to point out a variety of limitations to explanations related to the politics of age, and to this we now turn.

First, the politics of age may be less important in political systems that have passed the early birth pangs of modernization, but are not yet modern industrial societies faced with a possible postindustrial transition. In these, the political conflicts of modernization may be in full flower, especially those related to urban-rural differences, social class, and the like. The politics of age matter under some but by no means all circumstances. Stepan's Latin American study highlights this question. Although he finds that the politics of age are an important part of politics as linked to institutionalized military roles, he clearly does not claim that the politics of age are the most important way, or even a decisive way, to study many Latin American countries.

Second, political systems with strong conflicts along class or communal lines may not be so strongly affected by the politics of age. Alternatively, in issue areas shaped by class and communal matters, or for groups that feel strongly discriminated against, the politics of age may matter less. Age differences are set aside for the sake of class or communal action and defense. This is one of Kilson's principal conclusions in his discussion of blacks in the United States. Quandt also makes this point to distinguish the efficacy of age-linked and other kinds of explanations for different times and issue areas. Perlmutter, as well, underlines the importance of cleavages linked to religion and national origin in Israeli society.

Third, in "old" societies well past the founding of their most current political system, where there are important rigidities in the social structure, where ascriptive characteristics continue to be very important, and where political organizations may not be well institutionalized, we may witness a decline in the importance of the politics of age. As age-related founding issues are set aside, longer-lasting issues may assert themselves. No author in the volume addressed this issue explicitly, although the variety of outcomes mentioned by Isaacs and Quandt and the complexity of issues raised by Weiner suggest that this is a plausible hypothesis.

Fourth, competitive political systems, where class, religion, and other such conflicts are manifested in a moderate fashion and where the armed forces do not ordinarily rule directly, are also less likely to be affected by the politics of age, although parts of these societies may well be. Although West European political systems (and a few others elsewhere) were not discussed explicitly, Huntington raised this possibility comparatively through his discussion of the United States. He indicated that generational variables are probably of greater importance to understand politics in the United States than in Western Europe. Nevertheless, the differences between the United States and Western Europe on this point were the subject of some debate. Some invoked Inglehart's and other related research (cited by Samuels in the introduction to this volume) concerning Western Europe, where it appears that age cohorts after World War II possess different orientations that are consistent over time and succeeding each other. As this occurs, age cohorts alter the distribution of values in the political system. Thus the issue may be: Why do Western European countries (and Japan) become more similar to the United States after World War II in terms of the greater explanatory importance of the politics of age? It could be argued that there are a number of characteristics and factors common to industrial societies on the edge of postindustrial change that have reduced the conflicts based on social class and communal issues to a certain degree and have increased the weight of conflict based on the experiential generational model. Differences between the United States and these other political systems are likely to remain, for the reasons identified by Huntington, but they may have been and continue to be lessened.

If one is willing to entertain the thought that the politics of age play a role concerning certain issues, organizations, and political systems, then a critical question becomes what difference that does make. The politics of age seem to make a difference in four distinct ways.

First, as the maturation model would predict, the politics of age under certain circumstances are important in the allocation of social roles. As individuals become older, they and their roles change; the process of allocation of roles through age serves to insure macropolitical order and continuity. Elements of this sort of allocation process can be observed in the chapters by Griffith, Pye, and Perlmutter. They stress, in different ways and with different weight, and at times from generation to generation, important elements of continuity in the countries they study, but more generally they emphasize simply that the allocation of roles through age is an important and lasting characteristic of these countries.

Second, as the interactive model would predict, these same societies are also the most likely to experience bottlenecks caused by a generation that refuses to divest itself of its roles and may strike down younger challengers or harass them from retirement. These first two hypotheses, of course, operate not only at the level of entire political systems, but also within specific organizations. Thus they may also be pertinent to Stepan's studies of the Latin American military.

Third, as the experiential model would predict, the shared experiences of an age cohort, especially at a formative stage in late adolescence and early adulthood, may provide the basis for political consciousness, organization, and action. Much of what has already been said about colonial transfers of power and revolutionary situations can be associated with this hypothesis. In societies where ideologies and movements based on class or communal issues do not operate easily, conflict may take this form. As age groups are replaced in this way, the macropolitical distribution of values may also change.

Fourth, as none of the models identified by Huntington and Samuels may predict, the politics of age may tend to attenuate or lessen political conflict by providing crosspressures at certain crucial instances and by facilitating age links across groups that would otherwise conflict more seriously. Kilson's data on blacks in the United States indicates that for some purposes, older black people in the United States were likely to disagree with younger black people and to agree more with probable nonblack perceptions concerning necessary instruments of political action. Similarly, one link across the organizational diversity of Israeli society that may have contributed to social cohesion and to the lessening of certain types of conflict may have been the links through age. Pye's analysis of how generational layers cut across functional groupings in China has been linked to coalition formation and conflict; whether there is more lessening or more sharpening of conflict is not entirely clear in this case, but the matter is at least open.

When the interactive and the experiential models are at work, one possible result may not only be the politics of age but also the flowering of an ideology of generationalism. Huntington's study of the United States, and especially his references to the late 1960s, illustrates such a development in the United States. Some of the material presented by Isaacs and Quandt is at least open to the interpretation that generationalist ideologies may have operated in the cases they studied. Generationalism is an ideology particularly suited to the politics of opposition and to the politics of regime consolidation if a relatively young group of people seizes power. Its thrust is to demand that power be turned over to, or be consecrated in the hands of, a new generation. Arguments are put forth that the previous generation has failed and that they are discredited. Generationalism is inherently divisive; it is not a useful coalition builder on the way to power; and it thus may be somewhat muted in opposition groups that are actually successful. It is more likely to be used with success as an ideology of power consolidation than as an ideology to capture power.

This volume was intended to raise and explore, albeit briefly in each case, the possible utility of explanations linked to age. The nature of the endeavor did not permit a closer methodological challenge to some of the presentations. Thus, in concluding, it is important to raise at least some methodological difficulties. It is extraordinarily difficult to specify when an age group or a generation begins, and where it ends. Most empirical studies of the politics of age tend to settle for arbitrary cutoff points. Yet most theoretical studies bearing on these problems are not mechanically demographic; rather they address problems of consciousness, communication, and action. This problem renders a number of studies of the politics of age methodologically flawed.

Second, it is often extraordinarily difficult empirically to distinguish between the weight of age as a variable and the weight of other possible variables. Revolutions, colonial transfers, societal foundings, and similar major events are rarely carried out by people of the same generation alone; even when age groups are similar, generational consciousness may not be predominant. Are a young lawyer and a young peasant likely to be united to act because they are young? The answer need not always be yes. Class, religious, ethnic, and other considerations tend to play extraordinarily important roles. The risk of fallacy—attributing to the politics of age what is best understood in some other way—is very serious. Moreover, even when it may appear that the politics of age predominate, it is not always certain that they do. When students opposed colonial rulers, were they engaged in the politics of age, or were they engaged in the efforts by a new elite, possibly rooted strongly in class considerations, trying to seize power? When old people ask for more social security payments, is this the politics of age or the politics of poverty?

This is an exploratory volume; it is intended to resurrect arguments, to advance hypotheses, and to present some evidence on issues of long-standing significance. We have not discovered the importance of the politics of age—authors in classical antiquity and their many successors have done that—although we may have made a greater effort to relate age to political continuity and change. We have also not isolated the politics of age from other variables and considerations; on the contrary, all authors in this volume agree that generational factors do not substitute for analyses proceeding from different premises and using different approaches. We have attempted, however, to enrich our study of politics by considering a set of explanations that have been neglected in recent literature on political development. We have taken a very modest step to specify how one could further study the subject. Yet even some, such as myself, skeptical at the outset that there was anything of intellectual value in this endeavor, may have gradually become persuaded that this set of variables is worth exploring, that there are alternative explanations worth testing, and that, notwithstanding serious methodological problems, an understanding of the politics of age may contribute to an increase of our knowledge about continuity and change.

List of Contributors

Jorge Dominquez, Assistant Professor of Government, Harvard University, Cambridge, Massachusetts.

William E. Griffith, Ford Professor of Political Science, Massachusetts Institute of Technology, Cambridge, Massachusetts.

Samuel P. Huntington, Frank G. Thompson Professor of Government and Associate Director of the Center for International Affairs, Harvard University, Cambridge, Massachusetts.

Harold R. Isaacs, Professor of Political Science, Emeritus, Massachusetts Institute of Technology, Cambridge, Massachusetts.

Martin Kilson, Professor of Government, Harvard University, Cambridge, Massachusetts.

Amos Perlmutter, Professor of Political Science and Sociology, The American University, Washington, D.C.

Lucian W. Pye, Ford Professor of Political Science, Massachusetts Institute of Technology, Cambridge, Massachusetts.

William Quandt, Associate Professor of Political Science, University of Pennsylvania, Philadelphia, Pennsylvania.

Alfred C. Stepan, Professor of Political Science and Chairman, Council on Latin American Studies, Yale University, New Haven, Connecticut.

Myron Weiner, Professor of Political Science and Chairman of the Department, Massachusetts Institute of Technology, Cambridge, Massachusetts.

About the Editor

Richard J. Samuels received the A.B. from Colgate University and the M.A. from Tufts University. He is currently a doctoral candidate in the Department of Political Science at the Massachusetts Institute of Technology and is a Graduate Student Associate at the Harvard University Center for International Affairs. During 1975-1976 he was the Executive Secretary for the Harvard-MIT Joint Seminar on Political Development. He has done field research in Ghana (1972) and in Japan (1972-1973), and he has been named a Fulbright Scholar for 1977-1978, when he will be in Japan completing research for his doctoral dissertation on urban politics and local public policy.

DATE DUE

MAR 1 9 1981			